Introducing iOS 8

Steve Derico

Beijing · Cambridge · Farnham · Köln · Sebastopol · Tokyo

Introducing iOS 8

by Steve Derico

Copyright © 2015 Steve Derico. All rights reserved.

Printed in the United States of America.

Published by O'Reilly Media, Inc., 1005 Gravenstein Highway North, Sebastopol, CA 95472.

O'Reilly books may be purchased for educational, business, or sales promotional use. Online editions are also available for most titles (*http://safaribooksonline.com*). For more information, contact our corporate/institutional sales department: 800-998-9938 or *corporate@oreilly.com*.

Editor: Rachel Roumeliotis
Production Editor: Kara Ebrahim
Copyeditor: Charles Roumeliotis
Proofreader: Marta Justak

Indexer: WordCo Indexing Services
Cover Designer: Ellie Volckhausen
Interior Designer: David Futato
Illustrator: Rebecca Demarest

December 2014:   First Edition

Revision History for the First Edition:

2014-12-01:   First release

See *http://oreilly.com/catalog/errata.csp?isbn=9781491908617* for release details.

The O'Reilly logo is a registered trademark of O'Reilly Media, Inc. *Introducing iOS 8*, the image of Goeldi's marmoset, and related trade dress are trademarks of O'Reilly Media, Inc.

While the publisher and the author have used good faith efforts to ensure that the information and instructions contained in this work are accurate, the publisher and the author disclaim all responsibility for errors or omissions, including without limitation responsibility for damages resulting from the use of or reliance on this work. Use of the information and instructions contained in this work is at your own risk. If any code samples or other technology this work contains or describes is subject to open source licenses or the intellectual property rights of others, it is your responsibility to ensure that your use thereof complies with such licenses and/or rights.

ISBN: 978-1-491-90861-7

[LSI]

Dedicated to Frank Paul Romeo

Table of Contents

Preface

Why I Wrote Introducing iOS 8

I wrote this book for people with absolutely no programming experience. Most programming books assume the reader already knows another programming language or has a Computer Science degree. This assumption creates a large barrier to entry and increased confusion for beginners.

Introducing iOS 8 was designed for absolute beginners and serves as your own personal tour guide into the world of iOS programming. This book removes the confusing terms and jargon and replaces them with relatable real-world examples. It uses common occurrences like going to the grocery store, driving in a car, or eating at a restaurant to teach programming. Each chapter will explain concepts in clear, concise, relatable terms.

The goal of this book is to walk you from idea to App Store. This book will teach you the basics of programming, developing apps, and how to release your app to the App Store. No programming experience is required. You will learn to think differently and see the world from a new perspective. This book will give you the tools to change your life and the lives of others. *Introducing iOS 8* removes the jargon and intimidation from programming.

Who Should Read This Book

This book was created specifically for absolute beginners. No computer science or programming experience is required. Anyone can do it.

- This book is for anyone with an idea for an app.
- This book is for anyone who loves their iPhone or iPad a little too much.
- This book is for people who are interested in changing their life or the lives of others.

- This book is for people who want to understand the power of technology and how to harness it.

People from all different walks of life have used this content to make apps. Here are just some of the people I have taught to make apps:

- Designers
- Product managers
- Students
- Grocery clerks
- Baristas
- Stay-at-home moms
- Grandmothers
- Personal assistants
- Recruiters
- Investment bankers
- Doctors
- Lawyers
- Construction workers
- Bank tellers

You can do it, too, and I am here to help.

Who Am I?

I am Steve Derico, the founder and lead iOS Developer at Bixby Apps. Bixby Apps is a mobile app development agency located in San Francisco that builds top-rated apps used worldwide by millions and works with Fortune 500 clients like BMW, Lenovo, and MGM Resorts. You can find our work at *http://www.bixbyapps.com*.

After teaching a few friends and family members how to make apps, I founded App-School.com (*http://www.appschool.com*). App School is an online app development school for absolute beginners. No programming experience is required. App School has taught hundreds of non-programmers how to make apps. It offers live online classes, video chat office hours, forums, video tutorials, code examples, contests, and book updates. You can learn how to make apps at AppSchool.com.

I know the barriers and obstacles of learning to program because I have been through them myself. I have guided hundreds through the jungle as well. I am here to be your guide and help you build your very own iOS app. Please contact me, and I will respond.

- Twitter: *http://www.twitter.com/stevederico*
- Email: *steve@appschool.com*
- Phone number: (415) 779-2771

I enjoy wine, baseball, and running in my free time. I also love to hear from readers and answer their questions.

Navigating This Book

This book is organized to walk you from absolute beginner to your own app in the App Store. This book is best read from cover to cover in chronological order. If you do have some programming experience, I suggest reading from the beginning, as Swift may still be different from the languages you already know. This book covers Swift, a new language from Apple released in 2014. Swift is a young language, and will grow and evolve. Check for book updates and errata on AppSchool.com/book.

 You can register as an official Apple developer and learn more about Swift at *http://developer.apple.com*.

If you read a chapter per day, you'll have an app submitted to the App Store in less than two weeks. Hold on to this book as a reference after you have read through it from beginning to end. Each chapter will serve as a quick refresher when you come back to a particular subject. Some of the buttons and screenshots may differ based on your version of OS X. All screenshots in this book are taken using OS X Yosemite (10.10), but differences will be described for those using OS X Mavericks (10.9). Also, be sure to watch your capitalization and spelling when programming with this book. Capitalization and spelling matter!

Chapter 1, Getting Started
> Covers the basics of the App Store, setting up your Path to Success, and installing Xcode on your computer.

Chapter 2, Introduction to Programming
> Covers the basics of programming, including *Model-View-Controller*, and you will build your very first app.

Chapter 3, Diving into Swift
> Learn the basics of Swift, variable types, collections, and loops, and build a Tip Calculator.

Chapter 4, Diving Deeper
Learn about methods, objects, and classes, and build a Race Car app.

Chapter 5, Building Multiscreen Apps
Covers view controllers, table views, and navigation controllers. Build your very own Passport app.

Chapter 6, Next Steps: Debugging, Documentation, and App Icons
How to fix issues, learn from the documentation, and improve the Passport app.

Chapter 7, Devices and Auto Layout
How to make apps for different screen sizes using Auto Layout. Improve the Passport app.

Chapter 8, Maps and Location
Learn to use the GPS to find a user's location, create maps, and plot points. Build upon the Passport app.

Chapter 9, Camera, Photos, and Social Networks
Accessing the camera, viewing photos and videos, and adding Facebook and Twitter sharing to your app. Create an app called Selfie for taking front-facing photos.

Chapter 10, Running on a Device
How to run your apps on your iOS device. Build upon the Selfie app.

Chapter 11, Submitting to the App Store
How to set up the required contracts, create an App Store listing, and submit your app.

Chapter 12, Managing and Marketing Your App
How to manage your app once it is on the App Store, and how to update and market your app.

Appendix A
What is Objective-C, why you should know it, and how to read it.

How This Book Works and What You Need for This Book

Each lesson in this book is broken up into two distinct parts, lecture and exercise. The lecture portion will explain the terms and theories using real-world examples. In the exercise portion, you will learn by developing real-world apps like a Tip Calculator.

You will need a few items to get the most out of this book.

An Apple computer
You must have a Mac computer to develop for iOS. You cannot use a PC or iPad. Your Mac must also be running OSX Mavericks (10.9) or newer. If you do not already have a Mac, you can purchase one at *http://www.apple.com*. If you are on a

tight budget, you can buy a refurbished model directly from Apple (*http://bit.ly/ 1zmNQ4C*).

An iOS device

To build iOS apps, you must have an iOS device. This can be an iPhone, iPod Touch, or iPad. Your iOS device must be running iOS 7 or newer. If you do not already have an iOS device, you can purchase one at *http://www.apple.com*. If you are on a tight budget, you can buy a refurbished model directly from Apple (*http://bit.ly/ 1EPDyhn*).

Dedicated workspace

Learning to make apps is a different type of learning compared to learning history. Programming forces your brain to think differently and understand new perspectives. This type of learning requires a quiet area with no distractions. When you are reading this book, close your web browser, Facebook, Twitter, and Instagram. Dedicate a specific time period of your day just to programming. Only allow yourself to have Xcode open and dedicate learning time to learning.

Positive attitude

Learning to develop can be tough, but it can be incredibly rewarding when you create something people love or add value to someone's life. Times will get tough; remember: you can do it, and nothing is impossible. Stick with it and think outside the box.

Conventions Used in This Book

The following typographical conventions are used in this book:

Italic

Indicates new terms, URLs, email addresses, filenames, and file extensions.

`Constant width`

Used for program listings, as well as within paragraphs to refer to program elements such as variable or function names, databases, data types, environment variables, statements, and keywords.

`Constant width bold`

Shows commands or other text that should be typed literally by the user.

`Constant width italic`

Shows text that should be replaced with user-supplied values or by values determined by context.

This icon signifies a tip, suggestion, or general note.

 This icon indicates a warning or caution.

Using Code Examples

Supplemental material (code examples, exercises, etc.) is available for download at *http://appschool.com/book/*.

This book is here to help you get your job done. In general, if example code is offered with this book, you may use it in your programs and documentation. You do not need to contact us for permission unless you're reproducing a significant portion of the code. For example, writing a program that uses several chunks of code from this book does not require permission. Selling or distributing a CD-ROM of examples from O'Reilly books does require permission. Answering a question by citing this book and quoting example code does not require permission. Incorporating a significant amount of example code from this book into your product's documentation does require permission.

We appreciate, but do not require, attribution. An attribution usually includes the title, author, publisher, and ISBN. For example: "*Introducing iOS 8* by Steve Derico (O'Reilly). Copyright 2015 Steve Derico, 978-1-491-90861-7."

If you feel your use of code examples falls outside fair use or the permission given above, feel free to contact us at *permissions@oreilly.com*.

Safari® Books Online

 *Safari Books Online* is an on-demand digital library that delivers expert content in both book and video form from the world's leading authors in technology and business.

Technology professionals, software developers, web designers, and business and creative professionals use Safari Books Online as their primary resource for research, problem solving, learning, and certification training.

Safari Books Online offers a range of product mixes and pricing programs for organizations, government agencies, and individuals. Subscribers have access to thousands of books, training videos, and prepublication manuscripts in one fully searchable database from publishers like O'Reilly Media, Prentice Hall Professional, Addison-Wesley Professional, Microsoft Press, Sams, Que, Peachpit Press, Focal Press, Cisco Press, John Wiley & Sons, Syngress, Morgan Kaufmann, IBM Redbooks, Packt, Adobe Press, FT Press, Apress, Manning, New Riders, McGraw-Hill, Jones & Bartlett, Course Technology, and dozens more. For more information about Safari Books Online, please visit us online.

How to Contact Us

Please address comments and questions concerning this book to the publisher:

O'Reilly Media, Inc.
1005 Gravenstein Highway North
Sebastopol, CA 95472
800-998-9938 (in the United States or Canada)
707-829-0515 (international or local)
707-829-0104 (fax)

We have a web page for this book, where we list errata, examples, and any additional information. You can access this page at *http://bit.ly/intro-ios8*.

To comment or ask technical questions about this book, send email to *bookques tions@oreilly.com*.

For more information about our books, courses, conferences, and news, see our website at *http://www.oreilly.com*.

Find us on Facebook: *http://facebook.com/oreilly*

Follow us on Twitter: *http://twitter.com/oreillymedia*

Watch us on YouTube: *http://www.youtube.com/oreillymedia*

Acknowledgments

I couldn't have completed this book without the support from my family and friends. I want to take a moment and thank the people who made this possible:

Mom & Dad

Thank you for always believing in me no matter what. Thank you for providing me with the platform to succeed. I love you, and I am so proud to be your son.

Ben & Erica

To my brother and sister who love to keep me humble. You will always be my little brother and little sister. I will always be your big brother.

Veesta

To my wonderful, beautiful, passionate, smart, and hard-working girlfriend. You are always there by my side to support me through thick and thin. I couldn't have done this without you.

Grammy, Grampy, Nana, and Poppy

To the best grandparents in the world. You have given me enough love and affection for five lifetimes.

Friends: Steve, Andy, Jeff, Andy, Mike, and Mike

Thanks for being the most trustworthy and reliable group of friends. Go Irish!

Mrs. Rapp

The professor at Notre Dame Preparatory High School who brought me into programming my sophomore year. You opened me up to a world that I could call my own. I wouldn't be where I am today without your guidance. Thank you.

Jerry Baltes

My cross country and track coach at Grand Valley State University. Thanks for teaching me how to get better each and every day. Everything seems a little bit easier when I compare it to RoHo.

Gary Vaynerchuk

A big thanks to my favorite author and entrepreneur. You taught me if you want something, you have to take it. You also encouraged me to follow my passion and do what I love. Without this advice, I wouldn't be where I am today. Thank you.

Everyone who doubted me

Without you, this book would not be possible. I will never give up.

CHAPTER 1

Getting Started

In this chapter, you will lay out your path to success, learn the basics of the App Store, and get your Mac set up for iOS development.

Your Path to Success

Take a moment to plan your journey before you leave the port. Be sure to pack the following items:

Study the App Store

As you learn how to develop apps, be sure to take the time to study another asset you have at your finger tips: the App Store. It's important to look for trends and popular features on the Top Charts. Read the app reviews on the Top Charts each day and download new apps to see what the market likes and dislikes. This knowledge will give you an advantage over the competition.

Solve your own problems

Many great entrepreneurs got started building products that solved a personal problem. To start generating ideas for apps, consider building something you wish existed and go from there. The passion and consideration that you can draw from a personal issue will shine through in an app that solves that problem.

Watch people's habits

Next time you are on the bus or at a coffee shop, take a look at what apps people are using. This is a great way to determine the basis for a trend or new feature.

Practice makes perfect

Your first app won't be your best. Don't be intimidated by this fact or by other apps. Facebook has a large poster in their office that reads "Move Fast and Break Things." Take this to heart: this poster encourages the employees not to be scared of failure. The best part about software is you can always send an update.

Ship early, ship often

"Ship early, ship often" is a developer's mantra. This phrase encourages developers to get something meaningful on the App Store and add to it after that. Decide what is at the core of your app. Ask yourself, *"What value does this app provide? Does this feature help provide value? Do we have to have this?"* These questions will help to sort out priorities such as feature inclusion in a first or later version of the app.

Positive attitude

Learning to develop can be tough, but incredibly rewarding. When you create something people love or add value to someone's life, you can see that reward. Times will get tough; remember that you can do it, and nothing is impossible. Stick with it.

The App Store

iOS, Apple's mobile device operating system, powers iPhones, iPads, and iPod Touches. The iOS App Store opened in 2008 with just 500 apps. Over the last six years, the App Store has grown to over 1,200,000 apps. These apps have been downloaded over 75 billion times to date. The App Store can be accessed via the App Store app on every iOS device, or via iTunes on a Mac.

The Featured section of the App Store in Figure 1-1 contains hand-picked apps by Apple. These apps are showcased for a variety of reasons, including great design, new ideas, utilizing a new device technology, and more. The Featured section shows an overall list of featured apps by default. However, you can see featured apps for each category by tapping Categories in the upper left.

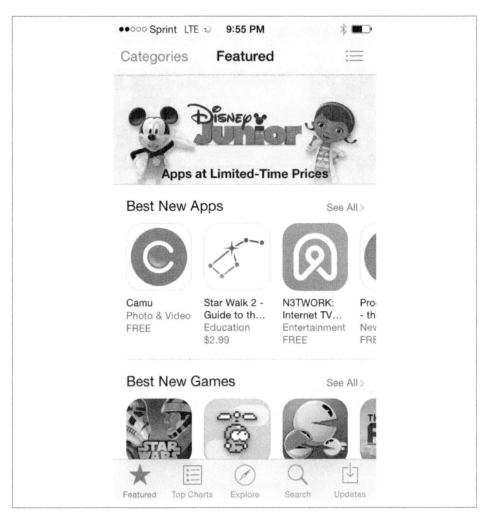

Figure 1-1. App Store Featured

The Top Charts tab in Figure 1-2 shows the most popular apps on the App Store. The Top Charts lists the top 150 apps in Free, Paid, and Top Grossing. Top Grossing apps are the apps that generate the most revenue. Most apps in the Top Grossing list are free and generate revenue through In-App Purchases. In-App Purchases are virtual goods that users can buy inside your app.

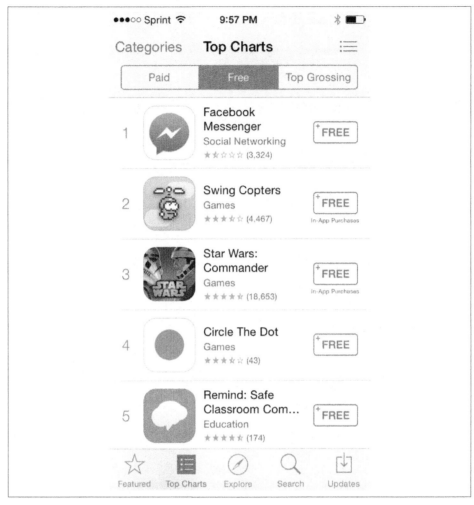

Figure 1-2. App Store Top Charts

The Explore tab in Figure 1-3 offers a different way to browse the App Store. The Explore tab allows you to browse deeper into a specific category and find related apps. For example, in the Explore tab, the Finance category has many subcategories like Featured Finance, Money Management, and Banking. The Explore tab will also recommend apps based on your location. This could be an app for the subway in New York City or an app for the Muni in San Francisco.

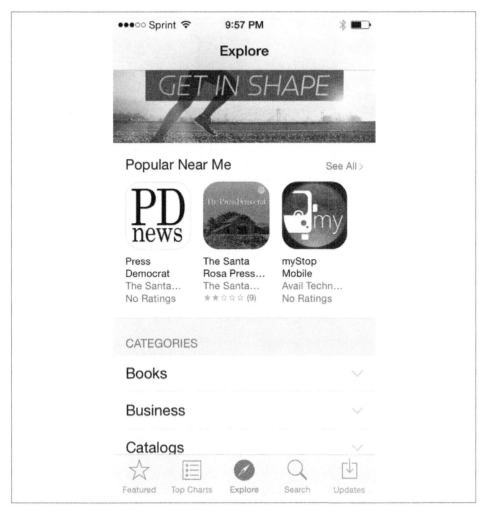

Figure 1-3. App Store Explore

The Search tab in Figure 1-4 on the App Store is where most users go to find their apps. When the Search tab is first opened, a list of trending searches is shown. This list contains popular searches by other App Store users. The search box at the top works like a typical search box. However, related searches or terms will be shown just under the search box as you type. Once your search is complete, a vertical list of apps will be shown. As of iOS 8, two screenshots will be shown for each app.

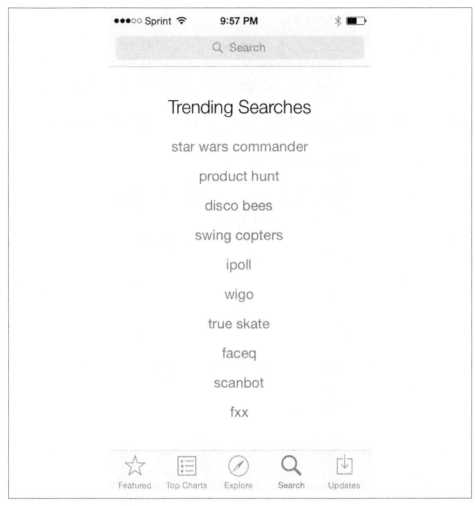

Figure 1-4. App Store Search

The Updates tab in Figure 1-5 will list all your apps that have recently been updated. As of iOS 8, the App Store will update your apps automatically. The top of this list also has a link to your previously purchased apps. Tap the Purchased button at the top of the list to redownload apps you have on another device or have deleted.

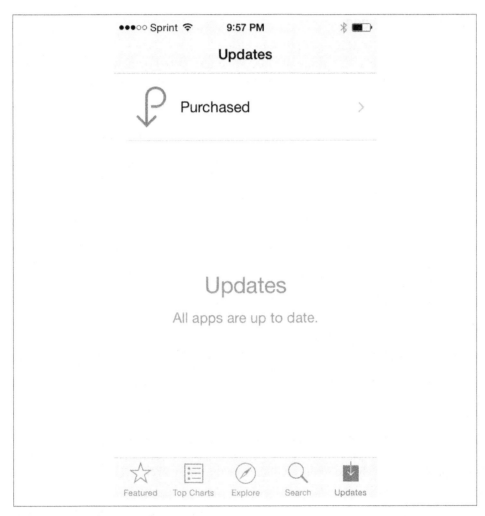

Figure 1-5. App Store Updates

How to Install Xcode 6

In order to develop apps for iOS, you must install Xcode. Xcode is Apple's development software created specifically for building apps on iOS and OSX. Xcode is completely free to download and install, and it only runs on a Mac. You will not be able to develop apps using a PC, Linux, or iPad. Xcode is like Microsoft Word, except it is designed for programming instead of writing. It provides many helpful features to ensure your code is working properly. Make sure you have the following items before you get started.

What You Will Need

A Mac running OS X Mavericks (10.9) or higher

You must have a Mac running OSX Mavericks (10.9) or newer. OSX Mavericks (10.9) is a free upgrade and runs on most Macs. You can update your Mac and read more at *https://www.apple.com/osx/*.

An App Store account

You must have an App Store account. This is also referred to as an *Apple ID*. Your Apple ID is the email and password used to purchase apps on the App Store, buy songs on iTunes, or sign into iCloud. You can sign up for a free Apple ID at *https:// appleid.apple.com*.

Administrative password for your Mac

Finally, in order to install and set up Xcode, you will need the administrator password for your Mac. This is a separate account from your Apple ID. This is the account used to log in to your Mac. If you don't have to sign in to your Mac, you're likely already the administrator. If the Mac is provided by your job or work, you may need additional privileges added to your account.

You can check if your account is also the administrator account by clicking the small apple in the upper-left corner of your screen. Click System Preferences→Users & Groups. The window will show the current user logged into the Mac and will say Admin just below the current user's name if it is the administrator.

Xcode is available on the Mac App Store and is a rather large download (over 4 GB). Make sure your computer has at least 5 GB of space free before you download Xcode. This process will likely take about an hour from the time you click download until Xcode is up and running.

If you haven't already started the download, click this link to the Xcode website (*http:// bit.ly/XUTt81*) or type the following into Safari:

https://itunes.apple.com/us/app/xcode/id497799835?mt=12

The Mac App Store should open up automatically. If yours doesn't, just click the blue button that says "View in Mac App Store." You will be redirected to the Mac App Store (Figure 1-6).

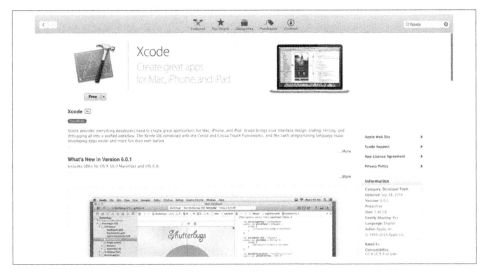

Figure 1-6. Xcode 6 in the Mac App Store

Click the silver button that says Free and then click the green Install App button. Then you will be prompted to sign in to your App Store account.

Your download will now start. Click the Purchases tab to track the progress of your download.

When you see Open next to the Xcode in the Purchases tab, the download is complete. Next, click Open, and Xcode will launch.

You may see a warning about opening a new program. Xcode will present the Xcode License Agreement. Read through this agreement and make your decision.

Next, you will be prompted to Install System Components; click Install.

You will then be prompted to enter your login and password. This is the password used to sign in to your computer, not the account used to sign in to the App Store.

The installation process will then begin. Once the bar is full, you are ready to launch Xcode.

Don't worry if Xcode did not install as expected. The best way to learn is to make mistakes. Practice makes perfect.

CHAPTER 2

Introduction to Programming

Programming can be a daunting concept, but it doesn't have to be. Most programming boils down to some basic math skills. No matter what level of math you have taken in the past, you will now learn the basics to get started. Before you start developing apps, it's important to understand how the magic happens behind the scenes. In this chapter, you will learn the basics of programming, how virtual objects are created, and some best practices to keep your code neat and clean. After you learn these concepts, you will put your knowledge to work and build your first app.

Learning to program is like learning to ride a bike. At first, the concept seems impossible, and you have no idea how to do it. It's not that you don't have the basic skills to ride the bike; it's that you haven't used those skills together before now. Programming is teaching your brain to think differently; the basic skills are not different, it's just a new concept.

Building Blocks

We are going to start to define the basic building blocks of a programming language. These are new concepts, and it is normal to do a double-take while learning them. They might sound foreign at first, but so did riding a bike.

Variables

When you check your bank account balance, it shows the current amount of money you have available. Your bank account may be $100 at the beginning of the month, and $350 on your payday. Since the amount of money in the account varies, the term "account balance" is used to represent the current amount. This is an example of a variable. A *variable* is a representation of a value. Variables come in many different shapes and sizes. Different types of variables hold different types of values. Variables can hold numbers, letters, words, true, false, or even a custom car.

Integer

An *integer* is a whole number, a number without any decimal places, positive or negative:

```
-10, 0, 100, 21031
```

An integer could be used for the number of stars for a movie review, a house's street address, or the score for a sports team.

Float

Sometimes, you need to be more precise with a value. In the case of currency, a decimal place is used to keep track of the cents on a dollar:

```
$10.51
```

A decimal-based variable is called a *float*. Float is short for *floating point*, another name for a decimal place.

Boolean

If someone asks you if the sky is blue, you would respond with either *Yes* or *No*. You cannot respond with 7, $103.45, or "Banana." This kind of *Yes* or *No* variable is referred to as a *Boolean*. Boolean variables are similar to a light switch—they are either *on* or *off*, *true* or *false*; there is no in-between value.

String

When someone asks your name, you respond back with a collection of letters that form a set of words:

```
"Steve Derico"
```

A *string* is used to represent characters strung together to make words and sentences. A string can hold a series of letters, numbers, and symbols. Strings are surrounded by a pair of quotes. For example:

```
"Steve is cool."
"Where is the ball?"
"Go Giants"
```

Classes

When you look at a busy road, you see many different types of automobiles. You see SUVs, sports cars, trucks, and sedans. Each type of car may look different, but every car has a few core characteristics. Every car has wheels, an engine, and brakes. Every type of car, no matter the brand, model, or style must have these core characteristics. Without these core characteristics, the car would not be a car. These core characteristics are called *attributes*.

A car is more than just a bunch of pieces of metal; it has a purpose and provides value to the consumer. A car can drive, honk, brake, and steer. These basic methods are available in every car. Without these methods, it would not be a car. These core methods are called *behaviors*.

If you were designing a new car, a blueprint would be a good place to start. A *blueprint* is a document that serves as a template for building something. The blueprint defines the attributes and behaviors of the car. A basic blueprint for a car might look something like Table 2-1.

Table 2-1. Car blueprint

Has Wheels
Has Engine
Has Brakes
Can Drive Forward
Can Stop
Can Steer Left and Right

The items beginning with *has* are the attributes. The items beginning with *can* are the behaviors. You can now use this blueprint to produce many cars in your factory, and each one will have the attributes and behaviors listed in the blueprint.

A *class* is a blueprint for a virtual object. A class defines the required attributes and behaviors. Just like a cookie cutter, a class can produce endless objects from a single blueprint. A star-shaped cookie cutter can create an unlimited number of star-shaped cookies. Each cookie will have the same shape as the cookie cutter.

Objects

If all cars have the same attributes, what makes a car unique? The values to these attributes make them unique. You might see a green station wagon driving down the road with standard wheels, a diesel engine, and standard brakes (Table 2-2). Then you might see a red sports car driving down the road with big wheels, a big engine, and performance brakes (Table 2-3). These cars each have different values for their attributes.

Table 2-2. Green station wagon

Wheels	Standard
Engine	Diesel
Brakes	Standard
Acceleration	Poor
Stopping	Great
Steering	Fair

Table 2-3. Red sports car

Wheels	Big
Engine	Big
Brakes	Performance
Acceleration	Great
Stopping	Great
Steering	Great

Each of these cars is an object from the car class. An *object* is the product produced by a class. An object has the attributes and behaviors from its class, in this case, the car class. The words *instance* and *object* are commonly used as synonyms. Keep an eye out for them, because people tend to use them interchangeably.

 Keep up with the list of synonyms in Appendix B.

You are an instance of the human race. There is no other human identical to you, even if you have a twin. Each person is completely unique. All humans have attributes like eye color, hair color, and a name. For example, see Tables 2-4 and 2-5, where the attributes are listed on the left, and the values are listed on the right.

Table 2-4. Person A

Eye Color	Blue
Hair Color	Blonde
Name	Larry

Table 2-5. Person B

Eye Color	Brown
Hair Color	Brown
Name	Magic

The combination of the values with their associated attributes is what makes an object unique. Humans have hundreds of attributes and thousands of possible values for each attribute. The permutations are endless, and as a result, each human is different from every other human.

Personal Challenge
What are some other examples of attributes for the human race?

Methods

Every morning when you wake up, you likely follow a simple routine of steps: get out of bed, take a shower, brush your teeth, get dressed, eat breakfast, head out the door. This routine of steps is very similar to how a computer works. A computer processes a list of steps to achieve a task. This list of steps is called a *method*. A method is a collection of code to complete a specific task. If you wrote a method for your morning routine, it might look like this:

1. Wake up.
2. Get out of bed.
3. Take a shower.
4. Brush your teeth.
5. Get dressed.
6. Eat breakfast.
7. Head out the door.

The method is executed every morning when you wake up. You know by the time the method is complete, you will be ready to take on the day. The completed result from a method is called the *output*. The input is what goes into the method, like an ingredient for a recipe, or a tree before it is made into paper, or in this case, your sleepy body.

Personal Challenge
Write down all the steps it takes to make a peanut butter and jelly sandwich. See how specific you can be.

Inheritance

Children often share the same facial features as their parents. *"She has her father's eyes."* *"She has her mother's nose."* The genes and traits of the parents are combined when the child is created. The parents' attributes and behaviors are passed down to the child. A parent and child may have similar attributes like hair color, eye color, or skin color. A parent and child may also have similar behaviors like the ability to play a sport. A father and son duo like Ken Griffey, Jr. and Ken Griffey, Sr. both possess the work ethic and physical traits to be professional baseball players.

The passing down of attributes and behaviors from parent to child is called *inheritance*. Inheritance is the ability for a class to extend or override functionality from a parent class. Imagine the car class you created (Table 2-6) was the parent of the SUV class (Table 2-7). The SUV class will inherit all the attributes and behaviors of the car class. The SUV will also be able to add its own attributes and behaviors.

Table 2-6. Car

Wheels	Standard
Engine	Standard
Brakes	Standard
Can Drive Forward	
Can Stop	
Can Steer Left and Right	

Table 2-7. SUV

Wheels	Mud
Engine	V8
Brakes	Standard
Drive System	All-Wheel Drive
Can Drive Forward	
Can Stop	
Can Steer Left and Right	
Can Drive Uphill	
Can Tow a Boat	

An SUV has wheels, brakes, and an engine. But it also has the ability to override the inherited attributes. *Overriding* is the ability to change how an attribute or behavior works for a class. This allows the SUV class to customize and control the inherited attributes and behaviors. Notice the SUV class has an engine, but it is a V8 engine. The class also has wheels, but they are mud wheels instead of standard wheels. The SUV class also has its own attributes and behaviors like an all-wheel drive system, the ability to drive uphill, and the ability to tow a boat. The child class is often referred to as a *subclass* of the parent class. In this case, the SUV class is a subclass of the car class.

Model, View, Controller

A closet is where you can keep all your shirts, pants, and shoes. A closet works best if you keep all of your items neatly positioned in different sections. This way when you need to grab a shirt quickly, you don't have to dig through your pants and shoes as well. Keeping your closet clean and organized makes using it much easier. Also, if you want to replace all your shirts, you can remove all the old shirts without touching the pants or shoes.

The same goes for your code. Writing clean and well-organized code will save you exponentially more time than digging through a rat's nest of code. The *Model-View-Controller* architecture helps to organize your code into three distinct parts (Figure 2-1).

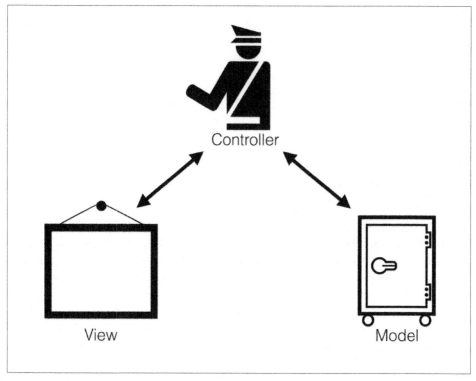

Figure 2-1. Overview of Model-View-Controller

Keeping your code organized will make it easier when you have to go back and change a particular section. It will also make searching and navigating through your code much easier. It's harder to change bad habits than it is to start new ones.

Model

The *model* portion of your code has to do with the data. For example, consider creating an application that stores all your friends' contact information. The model portion would hold the phone numbers and addresses. To remember that the model is the data, think of a safe containing zeros and ones (Figure 2-2).

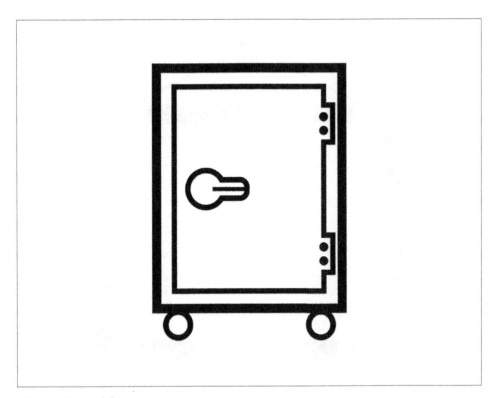

Figure 2-2. Model

View

The *view* portion of your code contains all the code related to the user interface. The view is like a picture frame; it holds and displays a picture, but it doesn't know what picture it is displaying (Figure 2-3). Your view code should not be connected to the content it is displaying. This way, if the interface is changed, it doesn't affect the content.

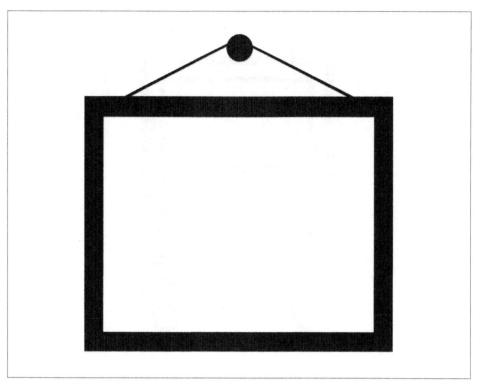

Figure 2-3. View

Controller

The *controller* portion contains all the logic and decision-making code. The controller is like a traffic cop; he directs the others where to go (Figure 2-4). It talks to the view and the model directly. The controller responds to taps on the screens, pulls data from the model, and tells the view what to display. The model and view never speak directly to each other. All communication goes through the controller.

Figure 2-4. Controller

Exercise: Hello World

It is time to start building your very first app. In this exercise, you will build a Hello World app (Figure 2-5). The app will have a button, which, when clicked, will display the words *Hello World* on the screen (Figure 2-6).

Figure 2-5. Completed Hello World exercise

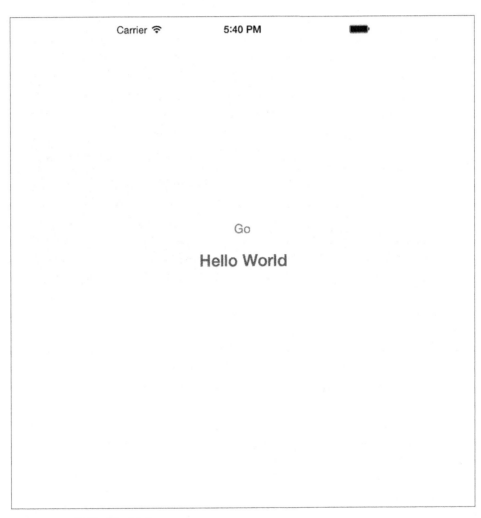

Figure 2-6. Hello World shown

The first step is to open up Xcode. If you don't see Xcode in your Dock, click the Spotlight search icon in the upper-right corner of your screen. Type in **Xcode** and click Top Hit (Figure 2-7).

Figure 2-7. Add Xcode to Dock

You will now see the Xcode icon on your Dock. Press the Control key and click the Xcode icon, hover over Options, and click "Keep in Dock."

Once Xcode is loaded, a welcome screen will appear.

Click "Create a New Xcode Project." Next, you will see the project template dialog (Figure 2-8). Select Single View Application and click Next. Then you will fill in some details for your new project (Figure 2-9).

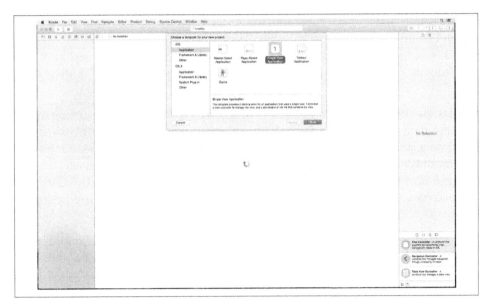

Figure 2-8. Project template dialog

Figure 2-9. Project detail dialog

The first piece of information is called the Product Name. This will be used as the name of the project and the name of the folder for the project files. Enter **HelloWorld** as the Product Name. The Organization Name is the company or person developing this product. Your first and last name with no spaces will work well for now. The Organization Identifier is used to create the bundle identifier. The bundle identifier is like the Social Security number for your app. This is the unique identifier that separates your app from the other apps. Your first and last name with no spaces will work well here as well.

The last two items are very important. Throughout this book, you will be using Apple's new programming language, Swift. Swift was announced in June of 2014 as the programming language of the future for iOS and OSX. Swift has many modern features that make a developer's life much easier. Set the Language to Swift; you can safely assume you will be working with Swift for the rest of this book. Finally, leave Use Core Data unselected, and under devices, select iPhone. We will cover the Device options in Chapter 7.

The next dialog box will ask where you would like to save your project (Figure 2-10). It makes things easier if you create a dedicated folder for all of your apps. Click the Documents folder on the left sidebar and then click New Folder in the lower left of the dialog box (Figure 2-11).

Figure 2-10. Save Dialog

Figure 2-11. New Folder name entry

Name the folder "Programming" and click Create. Finally, leave "Create Git Repository on My Mac" unselected and click Create (Figure 2-12).

Figure 2-12. Project details

You will see your Xcode project open.

The left sidebar is called the *Project Navigator* (Figure 2-13). The Project Navigator works like Finder on your Mac. It provides an easy way to explore and open the files in your project. The folders inside the Project Navigator are called *groups* and are not actual folders inside your Mac's file system.

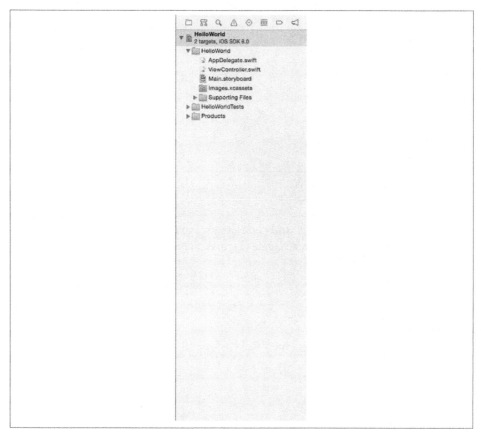

Figure 2-13. Project Navigator

The middle portion of the screen is called the *Editor*. The Editor displays whichever file is selected in the Project Navigator. Figure 2-14 shows the project details because the project is selected in the Project Navigator on the left.

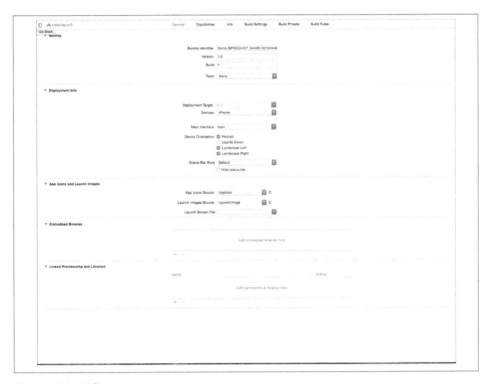

Figure 2-14. Editor

The right sidebar is called the *Inspector* (Figure 2-15). The Inspector is where details for whichever file is shown in the Editor can be changed. The Inspector is dynamic and will change depending on the file you have selected inside the Editor.

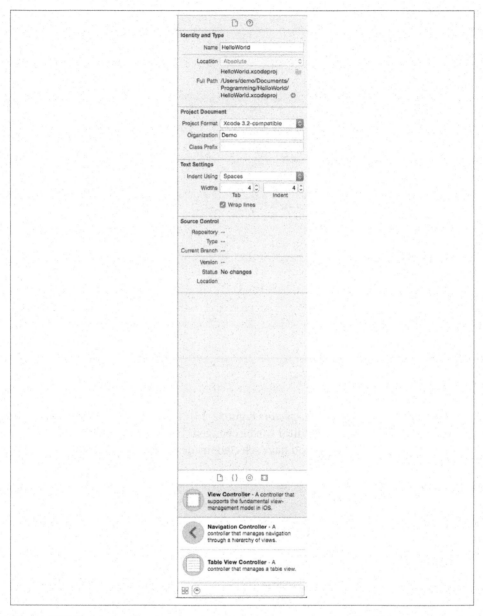

Figure 2-15. Inspector

The top portion of the Xcode window is called the *Toolbar* (Figure 2-16). It looks similar to the Toolbar inside of iTunes. In the upper left of the Toolbar, you will find the Play and Stop buttons. These buttons are used for running and testing your app. In the middle, you will find the Activity Viewer. This box will provide updates as your code is being processed. In the upper-right corner, you will find two sets of buttons.

Figure 2-16. Toolbar

 Remember, some of the buttons and screenshots may differ based on your version of OSX. All screenshots in this book are taken using, OSX Yosemite (10.10), but descriptions will be provided for those using OSX Mavericks (10.9).

The first set of buttons controls the Editor (Figure 2-17). The first button, with horizontal lines on it, will present the *Standard Editor*. The Standard Editor is the single view editor you typically see when you first start a new project. The next button, with interlocking circles on it, is called the *Assistant Editor*. If you are running OSX Mavericks (10.9), this button will have a small tuxedo on it instead of interlocking circles. The Assistant Editor will open another editor next to the Standard Editor and show files associated with the file currently displayed inside the Standard Editor. Think of the Assistant Editor like your butler, always at your side with the files you need. Finally, the last button is called the *Version Editor*. This view is used to track and analyze changes made to your project. For most cases, keep this on Standard Editor unless specifically told otherwise.

Figure 2-17. Editor controls

The next set of buttons, in the upper right of your screen, are used to hide or show the three major sections of Xcode (Figure 2-18). The first button will hide or show the Project Navigator. The second button will hide or show the Debugger. The Debugger will be discussed in Chapter 6. Finally, the third button will hide or show the Inspector. These buttons are especially helpful if you are working on a small screen.

Figure 2-18. View controls

Next, click *Main.storyboard* inside the Project Navigator.

The Editor is now displaying the Storyboard for your application (Figure 2-19). Storyboards are used to represent the user interface, or interface, for short. Storyboards hold all the buttons, graphics, and design elements for the application. Storyboards can stretch and scale to fit any size screen from iPhone to iPad.

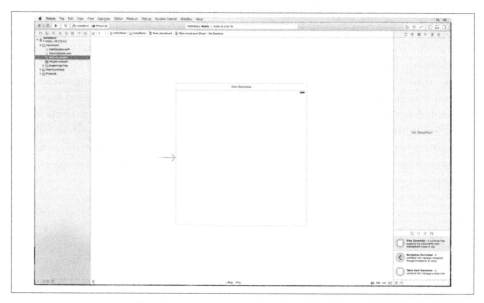

Figure 2-19. Main.storyboard

Your first app will run only on iPhone; click the first tab at the top of the Inspector. The tab looks like a piece of paper with a folded corner. About halfway down, deselect the Use Auto Layout checkbox (Figure 2-20), then select Disable Size Classes. Auto Layout is a set of tools used for multiple screen sizes and will be covered in Chapter 7.

Figure 2-20. Disable size classes

About halfway down on the Inspector is a small toolbar; click the third item from the left. The icon looks like a small circle with a square inside it. The icon will reveal the Object Library when you hover over it (Figure 2-21). Click the Object Library icon, and you will notice that the bottom of the Inspector will change.

Figure 2-21. Object Library icon

The Object Library holds the user interface elements you will use in your design (Figure 2-22). Scroll down through the Object Library until you see Label. A Label is a user interface element used to display text to the user. This text is only readable; the user cannot change this text. Click and drag a Label over the Storyboard (Figure 2-23).

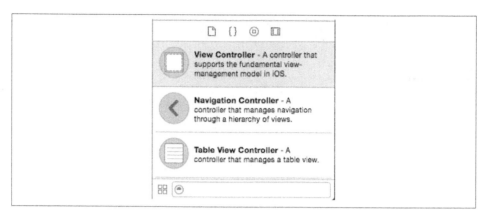

Figure 2-22. Object Library

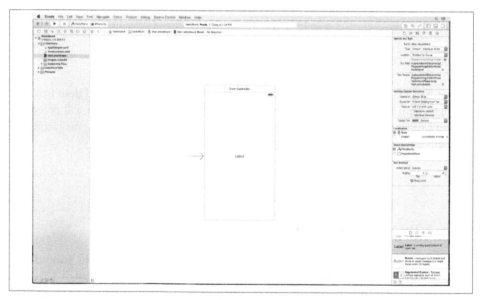

Figure 2-23. New Label

When you drag an element over a Storyboard, Xcode will help you snap the element to the horizontal center and vertical center. You may recognize this kind of assistance from desktop applications like PowerPoint or Keynote. Position the Label in the center of the screen. You will see the two guidelines when the element is in the absolute center (Figure 2-24).

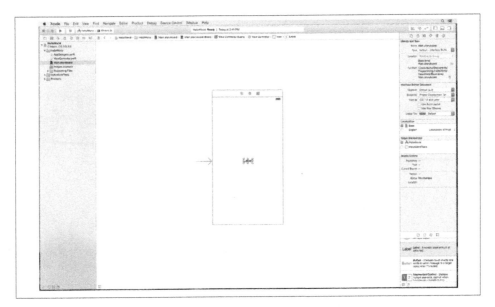

Figure 2-24. Centered Label

Next, select the Label and grab the white dot in the upper-right corner of the Label. Drag toward the upper-right corner of your screen. A small box will pop up displaying the size of your label. Drag until the Label is at least 150 pt wide by 30 pt tall and then release it (Figure 2-25). Recenter the Label as necessary.

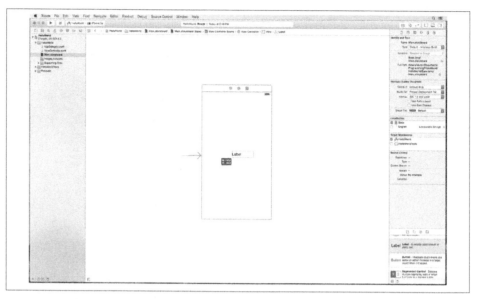

Figure 2-25. Resized Label

Once you have positioned your Label on the Storyboard, take a look at the Inspector toolbar.

Along the top of the Inspector is a small toolbar with six icons (Figure 2-26). Each of these icons represents a different section of the Inspector. Look at the fourth icon from the left. The icon looks like a downward facing arrow, and it reveals "Show the Attributes Inspector" when you hover over it. Click the Attributes Inspector icon. The Attributes Inspector allows you to change the values for attributes of the selected element on the Storyboard (Figure 2-27).

Figure 2-26. Attributes Inspector icon

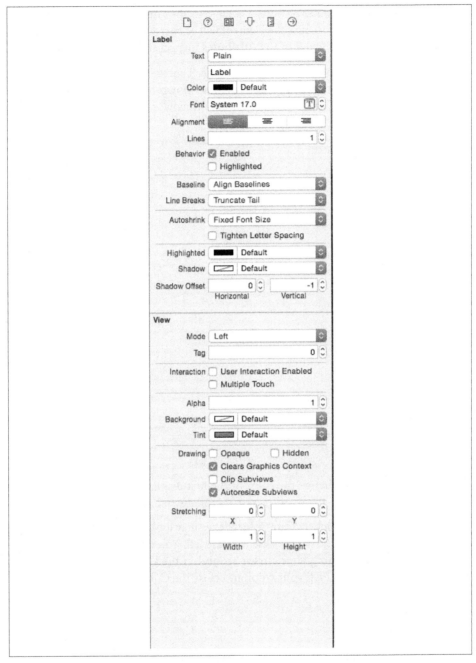

Figure 2-27. Attributes Inspector for Label

Click the Label and notice the options available in the Attributes Inspector. You can verify the Label is selected because the element will be surrounded by white dots, or you can look at the upper-left corner of the Attributes Inspector and see the word "Label."

Labels have many properties that you can change. The text attribute holds the string displayed by the Label. Underneath the Style drop-down menu is a text box with the word "Label" inside of it. Double-click the text and replace it with "????". Press Return (Figure 2-28).

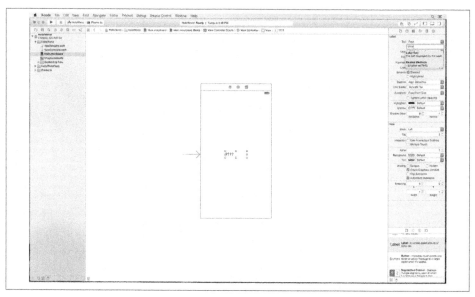

Figure 2-28. Updated Label

The color attribute will change the color of the text displayed by the Label. Click the drop-down arrows next to the word "Color." Scroll down and click Other.

This will present a Color Picker. Your Color Picker may look entirely black. If this is the case, grab the horizontal slider and slide it to the left. You will see a rainbow of colors (Figure 2-29). Click and drag your cursor around in the Color Picker and watch the color of your text change. Pick your color and close the Color Picker.

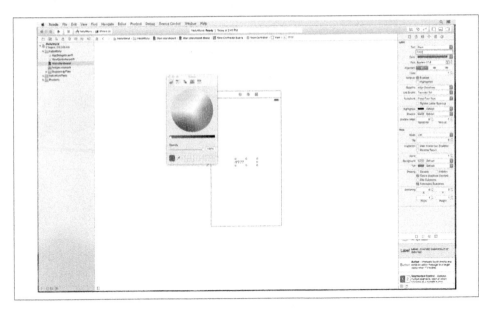

Figure 2-29. Color Picker

Turn your attention back to the Attributes Inspector and find the font attribute. Click the small box with a T inside of it. This will display a pop-up window. Click the drop-down arrows next to the font attribute and select System Bold (Figure 2-30).

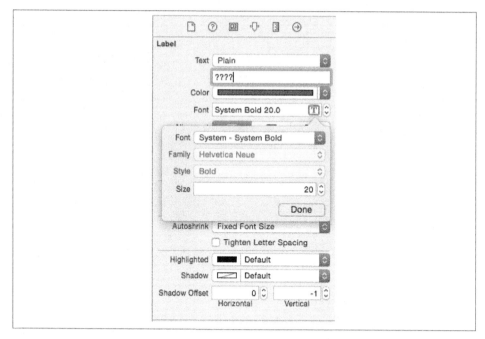

Figure 2-30. Font update

Click the small up arrow next to the size box and change the font size to "20." Click Done when you're finished.

Just below the font attribute is the alignment attribute. Click the middle button to center-align the Label's text (Figure 2-31). You may want to drag and recenter your Label after this change.

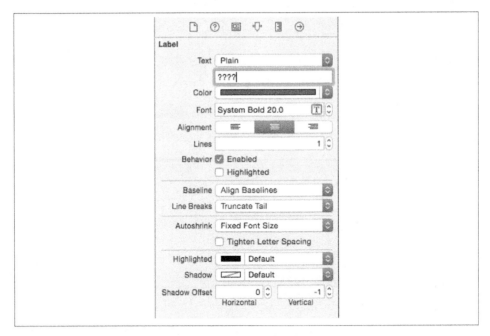

Figure 2-31. Alignment update

Next, head back over to the Object Library at the bottom of the Inspector (Figure 2-32). Scroll down and drag a Button onto the Storyboard. Position the Button just above the Label (Figure 2-33).

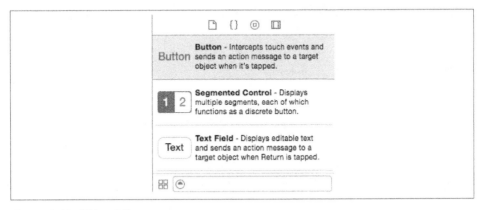

Figure 2-32. Object Library

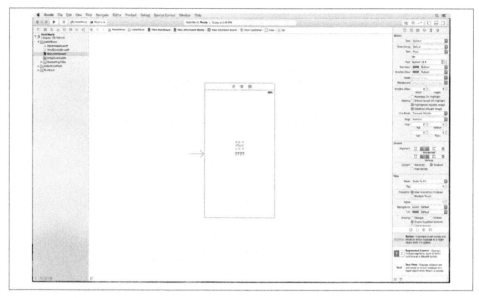

Figure 2-33. New Button

Double-click the Button and type **Go**. Double-clicking is a shortcut for changing the text attribute inside the Inspector.

Remember to always save your work. If you see a dark or dirty icon next to a filename in the Project Navigator, that means changes have been made but have not been saved (Figure 2-34). Click File→Save from the top menu bar to save your project (Figure 2-35). You can also save by pressing Command+S.

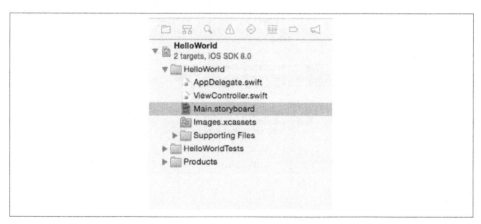

Figure 2-34. Dirty icon

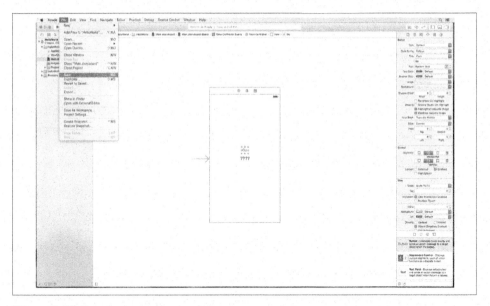

Figure 2-35. Save

You have finished designing your application; now you need to add some code that controls your application. But first, you must connect the interface elements to the code.

Start by hiding the Inspector. To hide the Inspector, look in the upper-right corner of your screen. Click the square button with a blue stripe on the right side of it. The blue stripe will turn to black, and the Inspector will be hidden (Figure 2-36).

Next, move your mouse to the left of the view buttons and click the button with inter-locking circles on it. If you are running OSX Mavericks (10.9), this button will have a small tuxedo on it instead of interlocking circles. A new Editor will appear on the right side of your screen. The Assistant Editor will detect what file you are working on and then display a helpful related file (Figure 2-37).

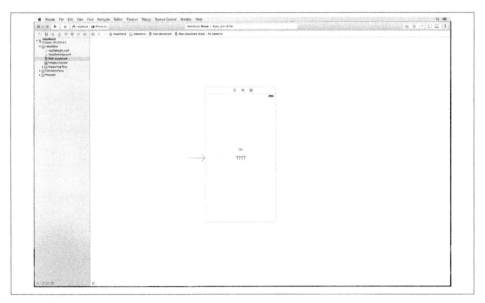

Figure 2-36. Hidden Inspector

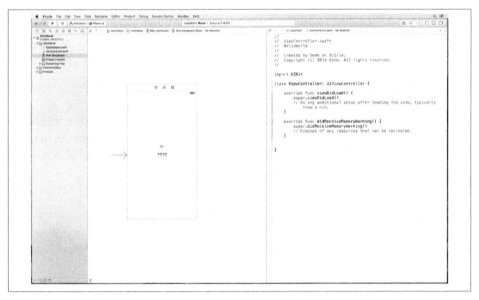

Figure 2-37. Assistant Editor

You may notice that it is hard to see the Storyboard, because it is hidden by another list of elements. This list of elements is called the *Document Outline*. The Document Outline provides a quick and easy way to select any element on the Storyboard (Figure 2-38).

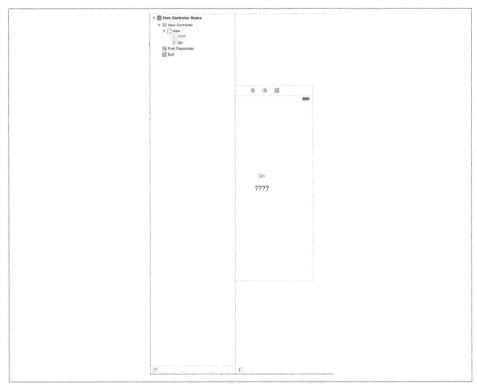

Figure 2-38. Document Outline

Look at the bottom-left corner of the Standard Editor and click the small square button with a stripe. This will hide the Document Outline (Figure 2-39).

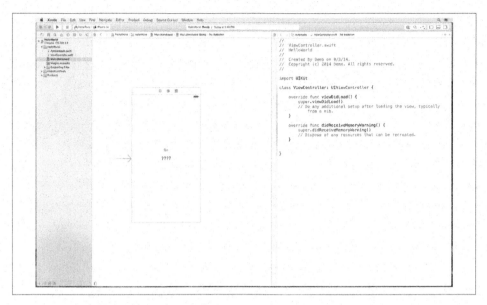

Figure 2-39. Hidden Document Outline

Storyboards

The Storyboard file is the view file in the Model-View-Controller paradigm. The Assistant Editor is currently displaying *ViewController.swift. ViewController.swift* is the controller in Model-View-Controller, and it holds all the logic for the interface you just created. Before you connect your user interface elements to your controller, you need to understand the two different types of connections between a view and a controller.

The first type of connection is an *action*. An action is triggered when a user taps, swipes, or makes a specified gesture on the interface. The action then sends an alert to the controller, where the controller can decide how to react. Actions are commonly used with Buttons. For example, a Button is tapped on the interface, and the controller is alerted. The controller can then choose what to do in response to the action.

The other type of connection is called an *outlet*. An outlet works in the opposite direction as an action. An outlet is a direct link to the view from the controller and is used to retrieve or set information from an interface element. For example, a Label on the interface has a corresponding outlet, allowing the controller to read and set the Label's text.

In order to create these connections between your view and controller, you will draw a line from one side to the other. Select the Label on the Storyboard (Figure 2-40).

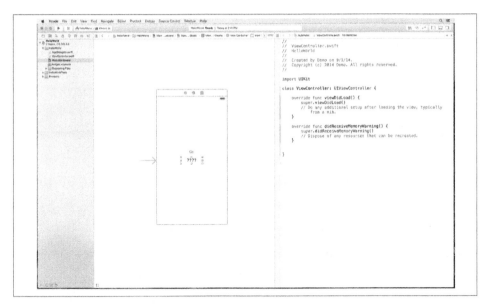

Figure 2-40. Storyboard with Assistant Editor

Now hold the Control key on your Mac; this is not the same as the Command key. The Control key will be on the left side of your keyboard next to the Option key. While holding the Control key, click and drag from the Label over to the Assistant Editor (Figure 2-41).

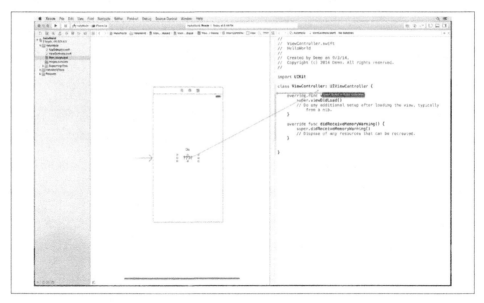

Figure 2-41. Control-drag connection

Drag your cursor immediately under the following words:

```
ViewController : UIViewController
```

When you see a dark blue horizontal line appear under your cursor, release your mouse. A pop-up window will appear asking you to enter more information about the connection (Figure 2-42).

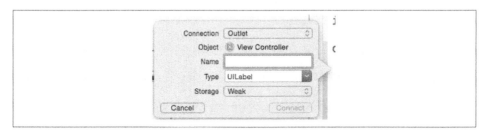

Figure 2-42. Pop-up connection dialog

The connection type is grayed out, and the outlet is selected. This is because a Label cannot create an action. For example, users cannot click a Label to do something. In the name field, enter **helloLabel** (Figure 2-43).

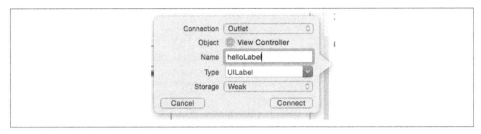

Figure 2-43. Completed pop-up connection dialog

 To use camel-casing, remove all spaces and capitalize each word. However, do not capitalize the first letter of a word. For example, number of years would become numberOfYears.

Always use camel-casing with outlet and action names.

It is best practice to state the class of element you are using in the name, in this case, a Label. This makes it much easier to tell which variable name goes to which element when you are inside the controller. After you have entered the name, click Connect.

Click the Button in the Storyboard (Figure 2-44) and Control-drag from it over to the same spot in the Assistant Editor. When you see the horizontal blue line, release your drag (Figure 2-45).

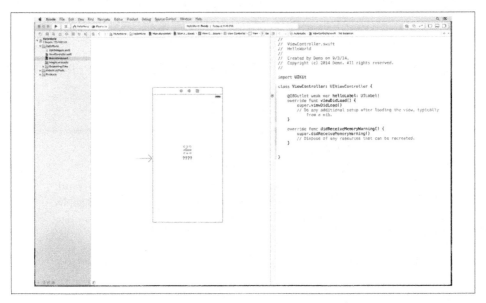

Figure 2-44. Selected Button

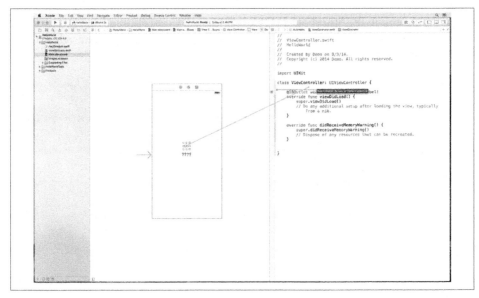

Figure 2-45. Control-drag connection

A connection pop-up dialog box will appear on the screen. Change the connection to Action. You will notice a new Event option will be displayed. This is the event that will trigger the action from the interface. Leave it on Touch Up Inside and enter the name **goTapped** (Figure 2-46).

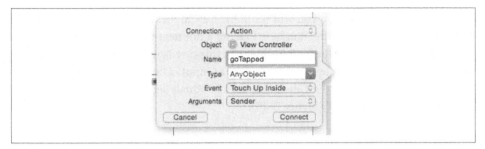

Figure 2-46. Completed pop-up connection dialog

It is best practice to name any action after the event that triggered it. In this case, Touch Up Inside means to tap and release your finger within the coordinates of the button. Be sure your connection is set to Action and click Connect.

The connections you created automatically generated some code inside the *View-Controller.swift* file (Figure 2-47). You will notice the keywords @IBAction or @IBOut let next to each connection.

```
//
//  ViewController.swift
//  HelloWorld
//
//  Created by Demo on 9/3/14.
//  Copyright (c) 2014 Demo. All rights reserved.
//

import UIKit

class ViewController: UIViewController {

    @IBAction func goTapped(sender: AnyObject) {
    }
    @IBOutlet weak var helloLabel: UILabel!
    override func viewDidLoad() {
        super.viewDidLoad()
        // Do any additional setup after loading the view, typically
            from a nib.
    }

    override func didReceiveMemoryWarning() {
        super.didReceiveMemoryWarning()
        // Dispose of any resources that can be recreated.
    }

}
```

Figure 2-47. ViewController.swift

Place your cursor at the end of the line that reads:

```
@IBAction func goTapped (sender : AnyObject) {
```

Then between the open and closed braces, write the following line of code:

```
helloLabel.text = "Hello World"
```

This is the only line of code you will write for this application. The variable `helloLabel` refers to the Label on the interface. Placing a dot next to a variable provides a list of the methods and attributes for this object. In this case, you are working with the `text` attribute. The `text` attribute asks for a string as input. The `text` attribute will display the provided string inside the Label. You use the equals sign to set `helloLabel`'s `text` attribute to "`Hello World`" (Figure 2-48).

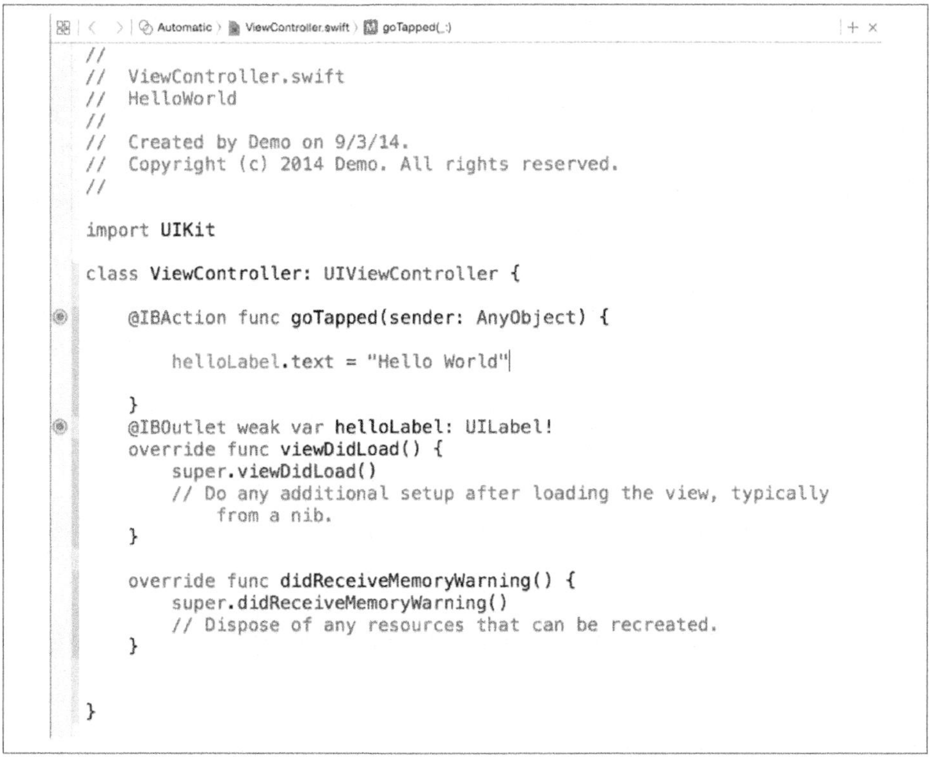

Automatic › ViewController.swift › goTapped(_:)
//
// ViewController.swift
// HelloWorld
//
// Created by Demo on 9/3/14.
// Copyright (c) 2014 Demo. All rights reserved.
//
import UIKit
class ViewController: UIViewController {
@IBAction func goTapped(sender: AnyObject) {
helloLabel.text = "Hello World"
}
@IBOutlet weak var helloLabel: UILabel!
override func viewDidLoad() {
super.viewDidLoad()
// Do any additional setup after loading the view, typically from a nib.
}
override func didReceiveMemoryWarning() {
super.didReceiveMemoryWarning()
// Dispose of any resources that can be recreated.
}
}

Figure 2-48. Hello World text

Now for the moment of truth. Click the Play button in the upper-left corner of your screen. You will see the iOS Simulator application launch with your new app. The iOS Simulator is a virtual iOS device that can be configured to be any iPhone or iPad size.

To run your apps on your own iOS device, you will need to register as an Apple Developer. This book will cover running apps on your device in Chapter 10.

The iOS Simulator may take a little while to load the first time (Figure 2-49). However after the first time, the iOS Simulator will load faster. If you don't see a virtual iPhone on your screen, check your Dock for the iOS Simulator icon. Once you see the app running on the iOS Simulator, click the Go button and bask in the beauty of your first app (Figure 2-50)!

Figure 2-49. Hello World launch

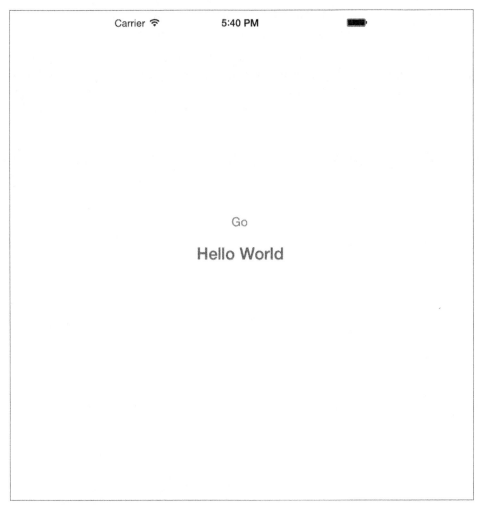

Figure 2-50. Hello World complete

If you made it through with no issues, congratulations. Now try to complete the entire exercise on your own without looking at this book. Memorizing the basics will make building apps easier going forward.

Don't worry if you received an error, a warning, or your app did not run as expected. The best way to learn is to make mistakes. Practice makes perfect. A sample version of the project is available on AppSchool.com/book. Download it, compare it, and try, try again. Don't be afraid to start the exercise over and walk through it until you get it right.

CHAPTER 3

Diving into Swift

In this chapter, you will learn the basics of Swift, Apple's new programming language. You will learn about creating variables, collections, loops, and conditions in Swift. These items are used in 99% of apps. This chapter will teach you the most important pieces of the Swift language, so you can start building apps fast.

What Is Swift?

Swift is a new programming language created by Apple as the language of their future. Swift was originally announced during the Apple Worldwide Developer Conference in June of 2014. Apple had used Objective-C, originally created for the Mac, for over 20 years. Swift was created to make writing code easier and more concise. Swift is perfect for beginners and has lowered the barriers so that anyone can make apps.

Playgrounds

One of Swift's most exciting new features are *playgrounds*. Playgrounds are a quick and simple way to write your code and test it immediately. I highly recommend that you keep a playground file open next to you while you read this book. Follow along and write out each line of example code provided. Writing out the code will not only help you see how it works, but it will also improve your muscle memory. Open up a new playground file now (Figure 3-1).

Figure 3-1. New file

Open Xcode and Select File→New→File. Click Source under iOS. Next, click Playground and finally click Next (Figure 3-2).

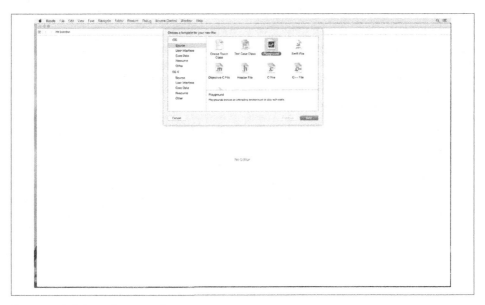

Figure 3-2. Select playground

Save your playground file after each chapter of the book.

Choose your Programming folder inside of Documents, created in the previous chapter, and click Create (Figure 3-3). You now have a playground file (Figure 3-4).

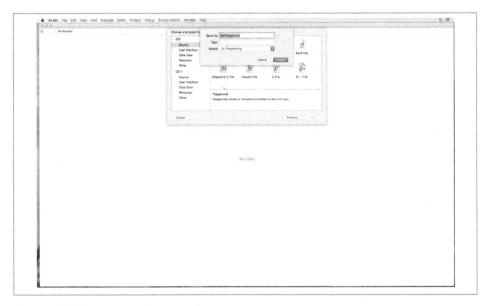

Figure 3-3. Name your playground

Figure 3-4. Playground file

Follow along with the example code from this book and experiment with your ideas. Experimenting is the best way to learn a new language. You can find the example code at AppSchool.com/book.

Creating Variables

Variables are used for values that will change, or are dynamic. *Dynamic* means that a value could change now or in the future. The `var` keyword stands for variable. This lets Xcode know you want to create, or declare, a variable.

Variables are referred to by their variable name. The variable name is linked to the value; that way, if the value changes, you still have a way to reference it. The variable name should be one word in camel-case. For example:

```
var numberOfYears
```

After the variable name comes a colon. This colon tells Xcode you are about to state the type for the new variable. A *type* is like a genre in film; some films are comedies, while others are drama, horror, or art films. Each genre has its own unique characteristics, but they are all films. To declare the type for a variable use a colon. After the colon, write the name of the type's keyword. For example, to create an integer, use `Int`:

```
var numberOfYears: Int
```

Finally, you must set a value to the variable. The value you set must match the type of variable you chose; otherwise, the variable will not be created:

```
var numberOfYears: Int  = 30
```

An equals sign is used to initialize a variable. *Initialize* means to set up or provide the default value to a variable. Think of it like unwrapping a new toy and forgetting to put in the batteries. The toy is useless until the batteries are added. You must initialize your variable with a value, or it will be effectively useless.

Integers

An integer, a whole number positive or negative, uses the `Int` keyword. The following line of code uses the `var` keyword to create a variable with `favoriteNumber` as the variable name. Then the colon is used to state the type. In this case, the type is integer, so the `Int` keyword is used. Finally, the variable's value is set to 4 using the equals sign:

```
var favoriteNumber: Int = 4
```

Float

A float, a number with a decimal place, uses the `Float` keyword. For example, this line of code uses the `var` keyword to create a variable and sets `accountBalance` as the variable name. Then the colon is used to set the type using the `Float` keyword. Finally, the variable's value is set to 1203.51 by using the equals sign:

```
var accountBalance: Float = 1203.51
```

Boolean

A Boolean, a variable with the value `true` or `false`, uses the `Bool` keyword. This line of code uses the `var` keyword to create a variable and sets `isStudent` as the variable name. Then the colon is used to state the type using the `Bool` keyword. Finally, the variable's value is set to `true` by using the equals sign:

```
var isStudent: Bool = true
```

Strings

A string, a collection of characters, uses the `String` keyword and is created with double quotes. This line of code uses the `var` keyword to create a variable and sets `firstName` as the variable name. Then the colon is used to state the type using the `String` keyword. Finally, the variable's value is set to `"Steve"` by using the equals sign:

```
var firstName: String = "Steve"
```

Remember whenever you are creating a variable, you must follow this format:

```
var variableName: type = newValueHere
```

Objects

Variables can also be used to represent objects. The keyword for the type is the object's class name. Remember, a class is a blueprint for an object. It contains all the attributes and behaviors for the objects it creates.

This line of code uses the `var` keyword to create a variable and sets `fastCar` as the variable name. Then the colon is used to state the type; in this case, the `Car` keyword is used to create a car. Finally, the variable's value is set to a new car object by using the equals sign. This example could work with any custom class:

```
var fastCar: Car = Car()
```

Personal Challenge
Make your own integer, float, Boolean, and string variables in your playground.

Constants

Sometimes there are things you are 100% sure will not change, like your birthday. For these situations, you use a *constant* instead of a variable. Constants are designed to work with values that will not change after they are set. Once the value has been set, it will remain that value for its entire lifetime. This consistent value is referred to as *static*. Static means the value will not change now or in the future.

Creating a constant is very similar to creating a variable. The only difference is that the `let` keyword is used instead of the `var` keyword. For example:

```
var numberOfYears: Int = 30
let name: String = "Steve"
let isMale: Bool = true
var bankAccountBalance: Float = 1034.20
```

You will notice the `name` and `isMale` variables are constants. These are items that will not change now or in the future.

You may be asking yourself, *"Why don't I just always use a variable and never change it after I create it?"* Well, that would work, but it goes against the best practices of programming. Best practices are recommended rules to provide a better experience for users and developers. For example, using a constant instead of a variable saves on memory and processing power. If all developers do this, it will make a better experience for the user.

Personal Challenge
Create your own personal variables and constants in your playground. How many can you think of describing yourself?

Type Inference

Declaring the type on each and every variable or constant can be laborious. The engineers at Apple are always working on new shortcuts to make developers' lives easier. Based on the value you provide on the right side of the equals sign, Swift can automatically detect, or *infer*, the required type. This is called *type inference*, and it simplifies creating a variable. Here is an updated example:

```
var numberOfYears = 30
let name = "Steve"
let isMale = true
var bankAccountBalance = 1034.20
```

The type and colon are no longer required, because Swift can detect the type of the value provided on the right side of the equals sign. Swift then automatically sets the variable's type to match the type from the value. This saves a lot of writing and makes your code simpler.

Modifying Strings

The `String` class provides convenient methods like `uppercaseString`, where the string is changed to its uppercase value. The `//` show the variable after it has been updated:

```
var favoriteFood: String = "Pasta"
favoriteFood  = favoriteFood.uppercaseString

//PASTA
```

When you set the `favoriteFood` variable to `favoriteFood.uppercaseString`, the equals sign takes the value from the right and applies it to the variable on the left. To break it out in steps:

```
1. favoriteFood //"Pasta"
2. favoriteFood.uppercaseString //"PASTA"
3. favoriteFood = favoriteFood.uppercaseString  //"PASTA"
4. favoriteFood //"PASTA"
```

Most code will execute sequentially. This means that the top line will run and complete, then the second line, then the third line, etc. The next line cannot execute until the first line is finished.

Personal Challenge
What happens if you remove line 3 from the playground? Why do you think this happens?

There is also `lowercaseString`, which changes the string to the lowercase version of its characters, not to mention `capitalizedString`, which provides a string with the first letter of each word capitalized.

Appending Strings

You can take a string variable and add on to the end of it. This is called *appending*:

```
var beach = "Beach"
beach = beach + "Ball"

//"BeachBall"
```

Strings can be appended with other strings to create new, longer strings. For example:

```
let firstName = "Steve"
var lastName = "Derico"
lastName = firstName + lastName

//"SteveDerico"
```

Or you can add string variables between other strings. For example:

```
let firstName = "Steve"
let lastName = "Derico"
var fullName = firstName + " " + lastName
var favoriteMovie = "Back To The Future"
var movieString = "My name is " + fullName + " and my favorite movie is "
+ favoriteMovie

//My name is Steve Derico and my favorite movie is Back To The Future
```

Variables in Strings

You can add variables directly into your strings using string interpolation. *String interpolation* is a term for creating a string with placeholders inside of it. Those placeholders are then filled in while the application is running. In this case, a string is created with double quotes. The placeholder is created with a \(). Inside of the placeholder is the variable to be inserted into the string. String interpolation is a very convenient way to convert a nonstring variable into a string:

```
let seatsPerRow = 25
let numberOfRows = 15
var seatsString = "In the theater, there are \(numberOfRows) rows and
\(seatsPerRow) seats in each row."

//In the theater, there are 15 rows and 25 seats in each row.
```

Collections

In some cases, it is necessary to hold on to many variables or constants in a container for better organization. Swift provides two collection classes that hold and organize your variables.

Arrays

What if you wanted to hold on to the name for each person standing in line for a roller coaster? You could create a variable for each person in line, but that would get cumbersome. You also don't know how many people could be in line at any given moment. To solve problems like this, you use an array.

An *array* is a container that can hold many variables in a specific order. An array can hold a nearly unlimited number of items and assigns each item a specific position value, or index. The *index* is the item's position inside the array. You can create an array like this:

```
var names: [String] = ["Steve", "Jeff", "Andy", "Andrew",
"Cole", "Mike", "Mikey"]
```

Start with the same var keyword, followed by a colon. Next, add a set of brackets with the type inside the brackets. On the other side of the equals sign, start your array with an open bracket. Inside the bracket, each item is separated by a comma. The array ends with a closed bracket.

Arrays in Swift must all have the same type. This means an array can hold all strings, like the previous one, but it cannot hold a mixture of strings and integers. Arrays can only hold variables of the same type.

Swift can automatically detect the type of variable for a given array. Instead of explicitly writing the type of variable, you can drop the type when you declare an array:

```
var names = ["Steve", "Jeff", "Andy"]
```

Navigating arrays

Each item inside an array has a specific position, or index. The index is just like a marathon race. *First, Second, Third,* etc. The trick to know about indexes is that they always start with zero. The first item in the array will be at index 0, the second item in the array is at index 1, the third item in the array is at index 2, etc. To access an item inside an array, use the following format. For example:

```
names[0]
//Steve

names[1]
//Jeff

names[2]
//Andy
```

It takes a little getting used to, but once you get used to it, you won't think twice about it. Indexes *always* start with zero.

 Personal Challenge

Create your own array with the names of your family members.

Use the count method to get the total number of items in the array. The index of the last item in the array will always be one less than the count:

```
names.count
//3
```

To check if an array is empty, or has no items inside of it, use `isEmpty`:

```
var cats = ["Big Kitty"]
cats.isEmpty
//false
```

Modifying arrays

Arrays that are declared with the `var` keyword are dynamic and can be changed as needed. To append or add an item to the end of your array, for example:

```
var names = ["Steve", "Jeff", "Andy"]
names.append("Wally")

//["Steve","Jeff","Andy","Wally"]
```

You can add another array to your array. For example:

```
var names = ["Steve", "Jeff", "Andy", "Wally"]
var parents = ["Mike", "Adam", "Nick"]
names = names + parents

// ["Steve", "Jeff", "Andy", "Wally", "Mike", "Adam", "Nick"]
```

You can replace an item in the array by accessing its index and setting it to a new value. For example:

```
names[6] = "Sam"
```

To place an item at a specific location, you can use the insert method provided by array. The insert method will move all items after the specified index up one position and place the inserted item at the specific index:

```
var names = ["Steve", "Jeff", "Andy", "Wally", "Mike", "Adam", "Sam"]
names.insert("Buster", atIndex: 2)

// ["Steve", "Jeff", "Buster", "Andy", "Wally", "Mike", "Adam", "Sam"]
```

To remove an item from a specific index, use the removeAtIndex method:

```
var names = ["Steve", "Jeff","Buster", "Andy", "Wally", "Mike", "Adam", "Sam"]
names.removeAtIndex(2)

//["Steve", "Jeff", "Andy", "Wally", "Mike", "Adam", "Sam"]
```

Dictionaries

Storing multiple items together in an array isn't the only way to organize your variables. Dictionaries can hold multiple variables and organize them using keys and values. These keys and values work just like *Webster's Dictionary* on your bookshelf. The key is the word you are looking for, and the value is the definition of the word. Dictionaries are not sorted or organized in a specific order. You must use the key to retrieve the value. For example:

```
var homeruns : [String: Int] = ["Posey": 24,"Pagan":19,"Pence":15]
```

In this example, there are three keys: "Posey", "Pagan", and "Pence". Each key has a corresponding value. Provide the corresponding key, inside the brackets, to access a value:

```
homeruns["Posey"]

//24
```

Add another key/value pair. For example:

```
var homeruns = ["Posey": 24,"Pagan":19,"Pence":15]
homeruns["Sandoval"] = 10

//["Posey": 24,"Pagan":19,"Pence":15,"Sandoval":10]
```

Replace an item by just setting the key to a new value. For example:

```
homeruns["Posey"] = 36

//["Posey": 36,"Pagan":19,"Pence":15,"Sandoval":10]
```

Remove a key/value pair by setting the key to nil. *nil* is a blank value and will be discussed further at the end of this chapter. For example:

```
homeruns["Sandoval"] = nil

//["Posey": 36,"Pagan":19,"Pence":15]
```

Loops

Imagine you are working out at the gym and your workout calls for you to lift weights eight times. You will be doing the same task, but eight times in a row. To handle repeatable work in programming, you use loops. *Loops* are used to repeat a particular section of code.

For-Condition-Increment

The most common loop is called the *For-Condition-Increment* or just a *for* loop for short. This loop has three pieces: a variable, a condition, and an increment. The variable is often an integer that is used to keep track of the current number of loops completed. The condition is checked after each loop; if it is true, the loop runs again. If the condition is false, the loop stops. Finally, the increment is the amount added to the variable every time the loop executes:

```
for (var counter = 0; counter < 8; counter++) {
  liftWeights()
}
```

The grammar, or *syntax*, of a loop begins with the for keyword. This tells Xcode you are going to create a loop. The for keyword is followed by a set of parentheses. Inside the parentheses are the variable, condition, and increment. For example:

```
for (VARIABLE; CONDITION; INCREMENT) {

}
```

The first piece is the variable. The variable is commonly known as a *counter* because it counts the number of times the loop is completed. It is very common to declare a variable named counter and set it to 0. For example:

```
for (var counter = 0;CONDITION; INCREMENT) {

}
```

Next, place a semicolon after the variable to separate it from the condition. The condition, in this case, is set to operate while the counter is less than eight. This will result in the loop executing a total of eight times. For example:

```
for (var counter = 0; counter < 8; INCREMENT) {

}
```

Add a semicolon after the condition to begin the increment. The increment is the code that updates the counter variable. For example:

```
for (var counter = 0; counter < 8; counter++) {

}
```

Most increments are written using a common shorthand practice. Normally, to increment a variable by one, the syntax looks like this:

```
counter = counter + 1
```

This code takes the counter variable and sets it equal to the counter variable plus one. This increases the counter value by one each time it is executed. However, Apple has provided a shortcut. Add ++ to the end of a variable name to increment it by one. For example:

```
counter++
```

This is the same as:

```
counter = counter + 1
```

for-in

Writing out a variable, condition, and increment can become laborious. The for-in loop was created to provide a simple way to iterate through an array or dictionary. The for-in loop automatically detects the condition and increment. Moreover, it creates a variable for you that represents the current item in the array. For example:

```
var favoriteStates = ["California", "New York", "Colorado", "Oregon"]

for state in favoriteStates {
        println(" \(state) is one of my favorite states")
}

//California is one of my favorite states
//New York is one of my favorite states
//Colorado is one of my favorite states
//Oregon is one of my favorite states
```

The println method, pronounced "print line," creates a string and displays it in the Debugger. The Debugger will be covered during Chapter 6. for-in loops can be used with dictionaries as well. To loop through an entire dictionary, you must list a variable name for both the key and the value. For example:

```
var homeruns = ["Posey": 24,"Pagan":19, "Pence":15]

for (name, hrs) in homeruns {
        println( " \(name) has \(hrs) Homeruns this season.")
}

//Posey has 24 Homeruns this season.
//Pagan has 19 Homeruns this season.
//Pence has 15 Homeruns this season.
```

Ranges

A *range* is similar to an array of integers from one number to another. There are two types of ranges. A *closed range* is written with three dots and includes the uppermost number:

```
1...5
//1,2,3,4,5
```

A *half-closed range* is written with two dots followed by a less-than sign and does not include the uppermost number:

```
1..<5
//1,2,3,4
```

You can use for-in loops with a range of numbers instead of an array or dictionary. For example:

```
for index in 1...5 {
        println("The current number is \(index)")
}

//The current number is 1
//The current number is 2
//The current number is 3
//The current number is 4
//The current number is 5
```

Conditional Statements

Have you ever been to a restaurant that sings to its guests on their birthday? Then you have been part of a conditional statement. A *conditional statement* is used to make decisions in your code.

if Statements

These decisions or logic can be defined using a conditional statement like an `if` statement. An `if` statement determines if a condition is true or false; if the condition is true, a particular section of code is executed; otherwise, it is skipped. For example:

```
if  isBirthdayToday == true {
        singBirthdaySong()
}
```

Conditional statements are written using the `if` keyword followed by the condition in question. In the example above, the condition is set to `isBirthdayToday == true`. The double equals sign is used to compare two values. If the values are the same, the result will be `true`; otherwise, the result will be `false`. If `isBirthdayToday` is `true`, it will execute the `singBirthdaySong()` method and sing to the guest. Otherwise, `singBirthdaySong()` will be skipped. Finally, open and closed braces are used to define the beginning and end of the code block.

if-else

At the end of a theater production or play, it is common for the actors to bow and actresses to curtsy. Each gender has its own specific action; each member in the production will either curtsy or bow, not both or neither. If you wanted to write this in Swift, it would look like this:

```
if isMale == true {
        bow()
}else{
        curtsy()
}
```

In this case, you check to see if `isMale` is `true`. If the variable is `true`, `bow()` will execute. Otherwise, the `else` keyword is triggered and `curtsy()` will execute. The top and bottom sections of this `if` statement are mutually exclusive. In other words, you can have one or the other, not both or neither.

Sometimes you need to check multiple conditions to determine what the next step is. When you wake up in the morning, it is common to have a routine for weekdays and a different routine for Saturday or Sunday. For example:

```
if isWeekday == true {
        getReadyForWork()
} else if isSaturday == true {
        goRunning()
} else {
        goToYoga()
}
```

In this case, you first check if today is a weekday. If today is a weekday, then you call getReadyForWork() and the if statement skips over the remaining sections. But if it is not a weekday, then the code skips the first section and goes on to the else if condition.

The else if condition is called if the first condition is false. If it is Saturday, goRunning() is called, and the remaining sections of code are skipped.

Finally, if neither of the conditions are met, the else block is called. The else block will catch anything the if or else if conditions did not catch. If it is not a weekday and it is not Saturday, then goToYoga() is called.

These if statements can be a very powerful tool in your programming tool belt. They can be used to control the logic and flow of your application. Remember that each condition you check for in an if statement must result in true or false.

Optionals

Optionals are variables that could result in the absence of a value. In some cases, it is not possible to know for sure if a variable will have a value. For example, a word in Spanish may not directly translate to a word in English. This means the variable could result in no value. This valueless state is called *nil*.

Optionals can be used with any type of variable and are explicitly declared using the ? symbol next to the type keyword. For example:

```
var translatedWord: String?
```

Since possible valueless variables must be explicitly stated, it is safe to assume all non-optional variables will have a value. This pattern is designed to help developers from accidentally working with a valueless variable. A nonoptional variable must have a value to exist. However, an optional variable can be valueless.

Optionals are not used directly. Before using an optional, it must be unwrapped. Think of using an optional like opening a piece of candy. You have to take off the wrapper before you can eat it. Remember an optional, when unwrapped, could be nil. This would be the equivalent of unwrapping your candy and finding nothing inside the wrapper.

The process of unwrapping an optional helps to remind the developer to check and make sure the variable is not nil. There are two steps to using an optional. The first step is to check if the optional is nil. This is commonly done with an if statement like this:

```
var translatedWord: String? = translate("cat")

if translatedWord != nil {
        //translatedWord has a value
} else{
        //The translatedWord has no value
}
```

Once you have verified the optional contains a value, you must unwrap it. Unwrapping an optional is as simple as placing an ! mark after the variable name. For example:

```
var translatedWord: String? = translate("cat")

if translatedWord != nil {
        println(translatedWord!)

        //gato
}
```

Optionals can be a bit confusing at first, but just remember a variable that could be valueless must be an optional. The valueless value for an optional is called *nil*.

In this chapter, you learned the basics of Swift. You can now create variables, constants, and even optionals. You are now familiar with how to create strings, integers, floats, arrays, and dictionaries. You understand how to create a loop and check conditions with an if statement. Now it is time to put your knowledge to the test. Keep up the momentum and build your very own Tip Calculator.

Exercise: Tip Calculator

Your next app will help users calculate how much to tip the waiter each time they are at a restaurant. The user will enter the total and then select from three choices for the tip rate: 15, 20, and 25 percent. The user will then tap the calculate button, and the tip amount will display on the screen. A screenshot of the final product is provided in Figure 3-5.

Figure 3-5. Finished Tip Calculator

Now that you understand what your app will do and how it will look, it's time to get started in Xcode. Click the Xcode icon on your Dock; if Xcode is not on your Dock, use Spotlight to launch Xcode.

Xcode will launch with a familiar welcome screen. Close the welcome screen and click File→New→Project from the top menu bar (Figure 3-6).

Figure 3-6. New project

Select Single View Application from the template dialog box and click Next (Figure 3-7).

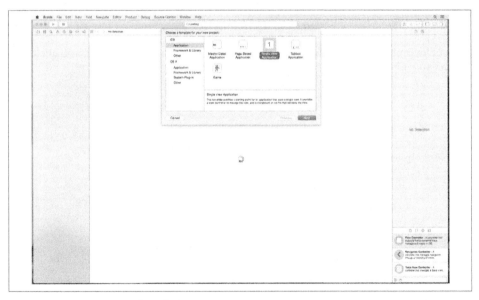

Figure 3-7. Project template dialog

Some of the project options may already be filled in for you.

Set the Product Name to **TipCalculator** and set Organization Name and Organization Identifier to your first and last name with no spaces. Finally, make sure the Language is Swift and Devices is set to iPhone (Figure 3-8).

Figure 3-8. Project detail dialog

Select Documents from the left sidebar, select your Programming folder, and click Create to save the project (Figure 3-9).

Figure 3-9. Save project

The project details will be shown (Figure 3-10).

Figure 3-10. Project details

Dive right into the interface. Click the *Main.storyboard* file from the Project Navigator (Figure 3-11).

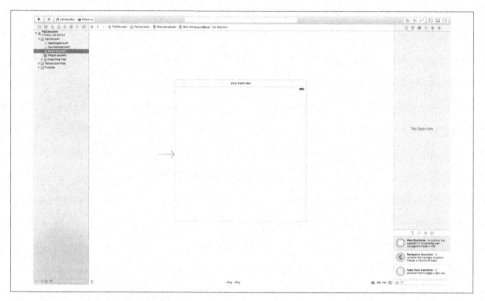

Figure 3-11. Main.storyboard

This app will run only on iPhone. Click the first tab at the top of the Inspector. The tab looks like a piece of paper with a folded corner. About halfway down, deselect the Use Auto Layout checkbox. A dialog box will appear; select iPhone and then Disable Size Classes (Figure 3-12). The shape of the user interface will change. Auto Layout is used for multiple screen sizes and will be covered in Chapter 7 of this book.

Figure 3-12. Disable size classes

Make sure the Inspector is showing on the right side of your screen. If not, click the Inspector View button. The Inspector View button is the square button with a stripe on the right side in the upper-right corner of your screen. This will show the Inspector.

Look for the small toolbar halfway down the Inspector on the right side of your screen. The Object Library icon should still be highlighted (Figure 3-13). If not, click the small circle icon that is third from the left.

Figure 3-13. Object Library

At the bottom of the Object Library is a small search box; type the word **Label** (Figure 3-14). The Object Library search box is a convenient way to find the interface elements you need, but be sure to clear your search once you are done. Otherwise, you will not be able to see the other available elements.

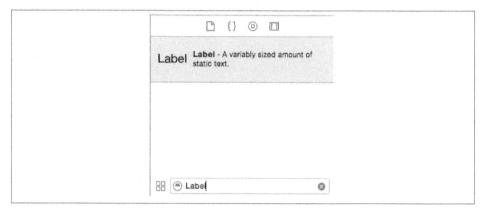

Figure 3-14. Label in Object Library

Drag a Label into the middle of the interface (Figure 3-15). Use the guidelines to help ensure you are in the horizontal and vertical center.

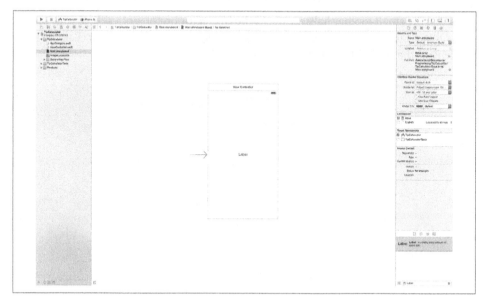

Figure 3-15. New Label

Look at the toolbar at the top of the Inspector. Click the Attributes Inspector icon; it is the fourth from the left (Figure 3-16). The icon looks like a downward facing arrow.

Figure 3-16. Attributes Inspector icon

Set the text attribute to **$0.00** and press the Return key. Then click the center alignment button (Figure 3-17).

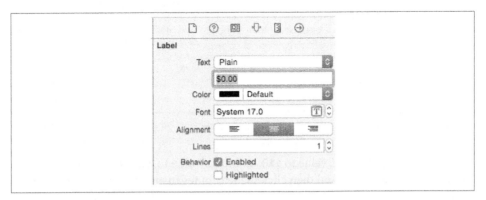

Figure 3-17. Label title

Look back to the top toolbar on the Inspector. Click the small ruler icon second from the right to open the *Size Inspector* (Figure 3-18). The Size Inspector helps to precisely set the position of an element on the interface.

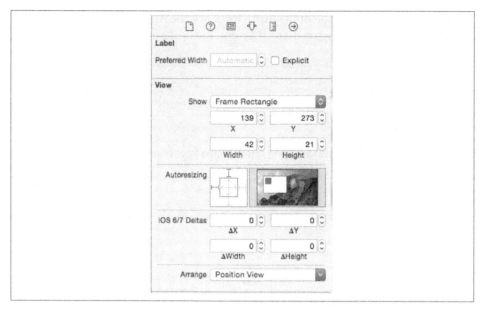

Figure 3-18. Size Inspector

Set the width to **100**, the X value to **110**, and the Y value to **200**. Notice the Label's new position on the interface and then click the Attributes Inspector icon (Figure 3-19).

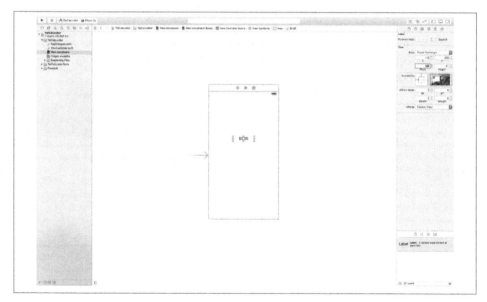

Figure 3-19. Repositioned Label

Next, you will add a Button to the interface. Move your cursor to the bottom-right corner of the screen. Click inside the Object Library search box and erase the word Label.

Scroll down through the Object Library and find Button (Figure 3-20). Drag a Button just above the Label. Be sure to keep it horizontally centered by using the guidelines to help position the element (Figure 3-21).

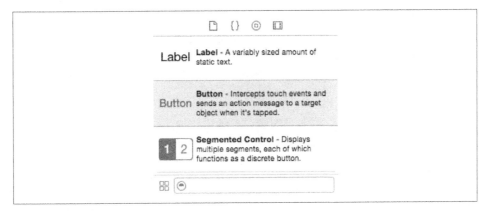

Figure 3-20. Button in Object Library

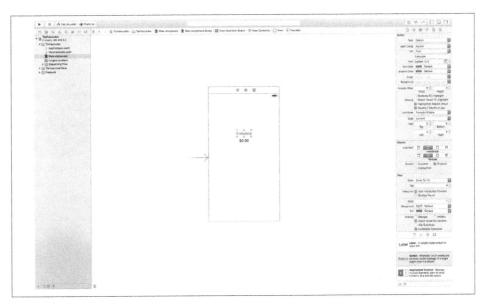

Figure 3-21. New Button

Double-click the Button, type the word **Calculate**, and then press the Return key.

Next, you will add a Segmented Control to the interface (Figure 3-22). A *Segmented Control* is like a light switch with more than two options. A Segmented Control holds two or more segments with action-like Buttons; however, only one segment can be selected at a time.

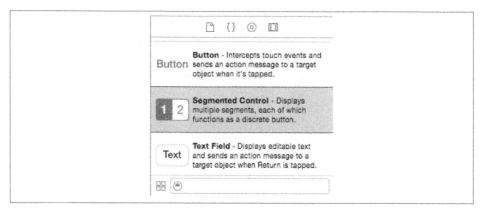

Figure 3-22. Segmented Control in Object Library

Scroll through the Object Library and drag a Segmented Control onto the interface. Position the Segmented Control just above your new Button (Figure 3-23).

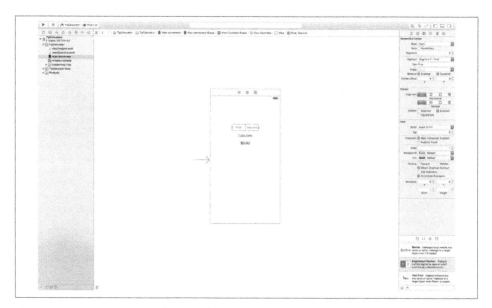

Figure 3-23. New Segmented Control

Verify that the Attributes Inspector is selected in the Inspector. Change the number of segments in the Inspector from 2 to 3 (Figure 3-24). You will see the Segmented Control expand on the interface (Figure 3-25).

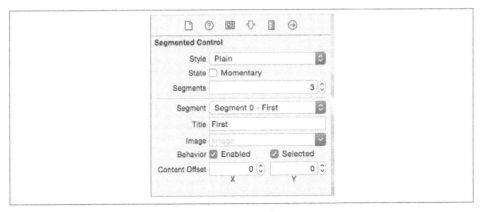

Figure 3-24. Attributes Inspector for Segmented Control

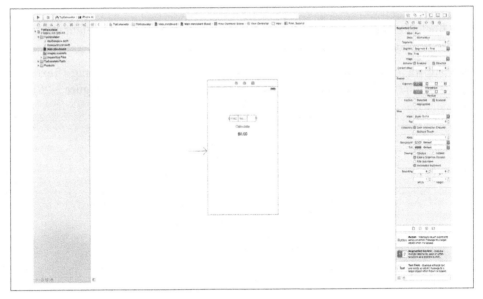

Figure 3-25. Three sections in Segmented Control

Next, double-click the word "First" inside the Segmented Control on the interface. The text will become editable; change it to **15%** and then press the Return key. Change the second segment's text to **20%** and then double-click inside the blank space of the third segment and set it to **25%** (Figure 3-26).

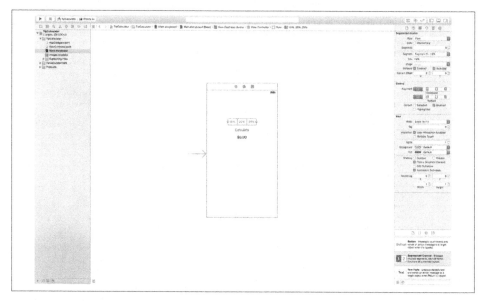

Figure 3-26. New Segmented Control titles

The final element to add to the Interface will be a Text Field. A Text Field allows the user to provide input via the keyboard.

Scroll down in the Object Library and select Text Field (Figure 3-27). Drag a Text Field onto the interface and position it just above the Segmented Control (Figure 3-28).

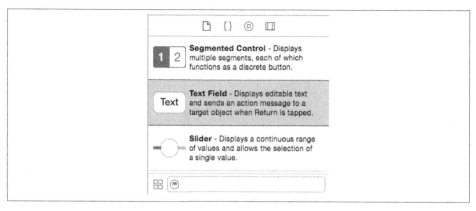

Figure 3-27. TextField in Object Library

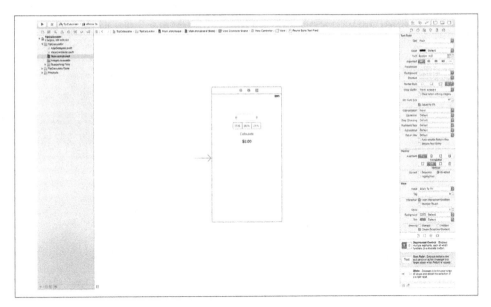

Figure 3-28. New Text Field

Turn to the Attributes Inspector and find the Placeholder attribute; it is the fifth attribute from the top. Enter the text **Total Bill $** (Figure 3-29). This placeholder text will serve as a guide to users before they tap inside the Text Field.

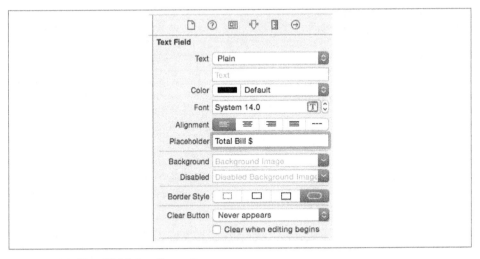

Figure 3-29. Text Field Attributes Inspector

Once the user taps inside the Text Field, the placeholder text will be cleared, and the keyboard will appear from the bottom of the screen.

Next, scroll down the Inspector until you find the Keyboard Type attribute. Click the drop-down arrows next to the word Default and select Decimal Pad (Figure 3-30). This will present a keyboard with only numbers, so your users will not be able to type letters into the Text Field.

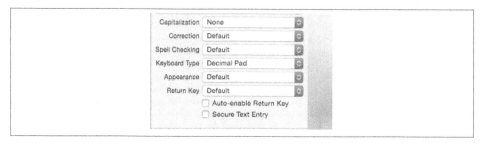

Figure 3-30. Text Field keyboard

The interface is now complete. Now it is time to connect the view, your user interface, to the controller, which is your Swift file. Just like the last exercise, you will use the Assistant Editor to help draw your connections between the view and controller.

In the upper-right corner of the screen, click the Assistant Editor button (Figure 3-31). This will open the Assistant Editor on the right side of your screen. To clean up more space, hide the Inspector by clicking the Inspector View button in the upper-right corner of your screen (Figure 3-32).

Figure 3-31. Assistant Editor button

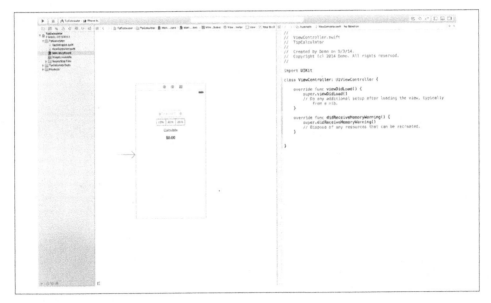

Figure 3-32. Hidden Inspector

The Assistant Editor will open the *ViewController.swift* file automatically. You can verify this by checking the filename shown at the top of the Assistant Editor, right next to the word "Automatic."

Select the Text Field element on the Interface. While holding the Control key, click and drag from the Text Field to below the words:

```
class ViewController: UIViewController {
```

Release your mouse when you see a blue horizontal line (Figure 3-33) and then a pop-up dialog will be shown (Figure 3-34).

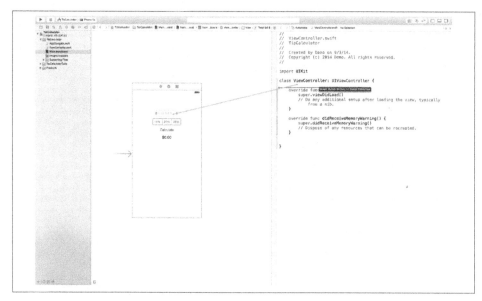

Figure 3-33. Control-drag connection

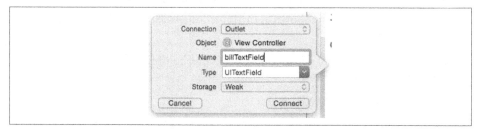

Figure 3-34. Pop-up connection dialog

Since you will be retrieving a value from the Text Field, you will use the Outlet connection type. Enter **billTextField** for the variable name and leave the remaining values as UITextField and Weak. Click Connect when finished.

The connection generated code when you clicked the Connect button (Figure 3-35). Take a look at the generated code:

```
@IBOutlet var billTextField : UITextField!
```

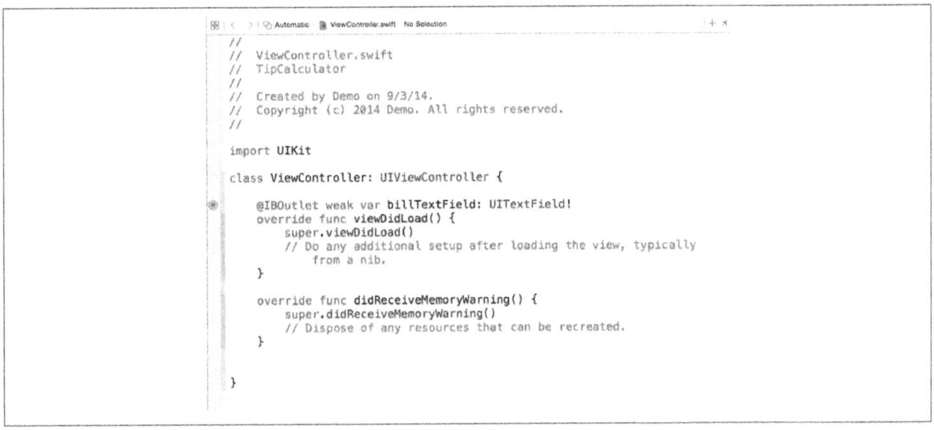

```
//
//  ViewController.swift
//  TipCalculator
//
//  Created by Demo on 9/3/14.
//  Copyright (c) 2014 Demo. All rights reserved.
//

import UIKit

class ViewController: UIViewController {

    @IBOutlet weak var billTextField: UITextField!
    override func viewDidLoad() {
        super.viewDidLoad()
        // Do any additional setup after loading the view, typically
            from a nib.
    }

    override func didReceiveMemoryWarning() {
        super.didReceiveMemoryWarning()
        // Dispose of any resources that can be recreated.
    }

}
```

Figure 3-35. ViewController.swift

Skip over the first word and come back to it later. You know the `var` keyword is used to declare a variable. `billTextField` is the name of your new variable, the colon is used to designate the type of variable, and the `UITextField` is the type. Finally, the `@IBOutlet` keyword is used to declare an outlet connection between the view and controller. The new `billTextField` variable will be used to reference the Text Field from your code.

Select the Segmented Control on the interface. While holding the Control key, click and drag from the interface to just below the following words:

```
class ViewController: UIViewController {
```

Release your mouse when you see a blue horizontal line (Figure 3-36); a pop-up dialog will be shown (Figure 3-37).

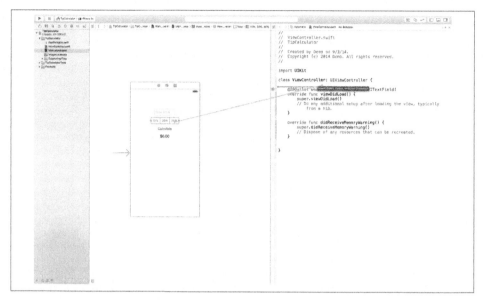

Figure 3-36. Control-drag connection

Figure 3-37. Pop-up connection dialog

Set the Connection type to Outlet. Name the connection **tipRateSegmentedControl**. Leave the rest of the options as they are and click Connect.

Select the Label on the interface. While holding the Control key, click and drag from the interface to just below the following words:

```
class ViewController: UIViewController {
```

Release your mouse when you see a blue horizontal line (Figure 3-38); a pop-up dialog will be shown (Figure 3-39).

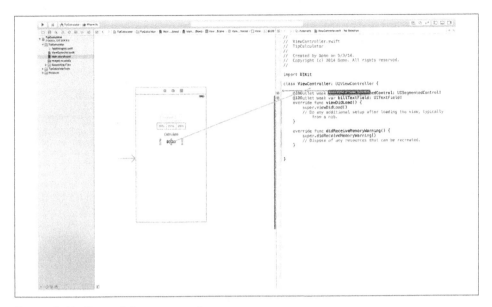

Figure 3-38. Control-drag connection

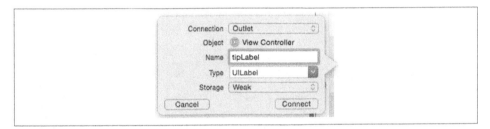

Figure 3-39. Pop-up connection dialog

Set the Connection type to Outlet. Name the connection **tipLabel**. Leave the rest of the options as they are and click Connect.

Finally, select the Button on the interface. While holding the Control key, click and drag from the interface to just below the following words:

```
class ViewController: UIViewController {
```

Release your mouse when you see a blue horizontal line (Figure 3-40); a pop-up dialog will be shown (Figure 3-41).

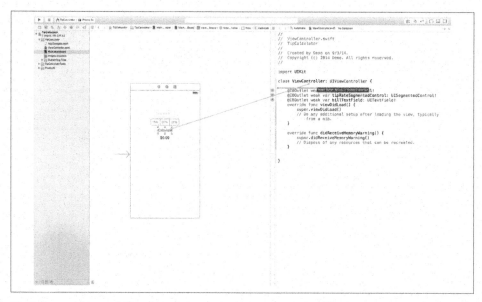

Figure 3-40. Control-drag connection

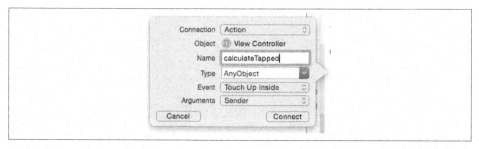

Figure 3-41. Pop-up connection dialog

Set the Connection type to Action. Name the connection **calculateTapped**. Leave the rest of the options as they are and click Connect.

The following code has been added to your *ViewController.swift* file:

```
@IBOutlet var tipLabel : UILabel!
@IBOutlet var tipRateSegmentedControl : UISegmentedControl!
@IBOutlet var billTextField : UITextField!

@IBAction func calculateTapped(sender : AnyObject) {

}
```

The calculateTapped action automatically created a method that will be called every time the Calculate button is tapped. Place your cursor between the braces of the calculateTapped method.

It's best practice to write notes that explain what you would like to accomplish before writing it in code. This process, called *pseudocoding*, helps to map the idea of a particular method before it is implemented. You can use comments to write notes directly inside of Xcode. Comments are also used to inform other developers about the code. Comments are not seen by Xcode when the app is running or being built.

To create a comment, write two forward slashes and then your message. For example:

```
@IBAction func calculateTapped(sender : AnyObject) {
        //This code is run each time the Calculate Button is tapped.

}
```

Add the following comments to the calculateTapped method:

```
@IBAction func calculateTapped(sender : AnyObject) {
//1. Get the total bill
//2. Determine the tip rate
//3. Calculate the Tip
//4. Display the Tip

}
```

Next, you will determine the tip rate: 15%, 20%, or 25%. Once you have the tip rate, you will multiply the total bill by the tip rate to calculate the tip. Finally, you will display the tip to the user.

Now that you have set the plan for your method, go through and write the code for each step inside the calculateTapped method.

To get the total bill, you will use the text attribute from the Text Field variable billTextField. Place your cursor at the end of the first comment and press the Return key. Then type the following:

```
var userInput = billTextField.text as NSString
```

Notice that while you are typing, Xcode will provide words to help you write your code. For example, delete the ".text" from billTextField and type `.`.

This predictive typing system is called *Autocomplete*. Autocomplete can dramatically improve a developer's experience. The Autocomplete pop-up will show you all the attributes and methods available for a particular variable.

After the `billTextField.`, type **te**. Autocomplete will update as you type and present the `text` attribute. Autocomplete even shows you that the `text` attribute will return a string; press the Tab key to accept.

You have now captured the text from the user in the Text Field. However, the `text` attribute from Text Field provides a string. You cannot complete mathematics with a set of characters. You will need to convert your string into a float. Remember, a float is a number with a decimal place. This will serve you perfectly for dealing with currency. To convert the string to a float, write the following on the next line:

```
var totalBill: Float = userInput.floatValue
```

This line of code creates a new variable using the `var` keyword and assigns it a name, `totalBill`, and then sets the type to float. Your new `totalBill` variable is set to `user Input` converted to a float, using the `floatValue` method. Step 1 is complete.

Your next step is to determine the tip rate. You will determine the tip rate by detecting which of the three segments is selected on the Segmented Control. Segmented Controls have an attribute called `selectedSegmentIndex` that provides a position representing the selected segment. Add the following code under the second comment:

```
var index: Int = tipRateSegmentedControl.selectedSegmentIndex
```

This code creates a new variable called `index` and sets itself equal to the `tipRateSeg mentedControl`'s selected segment. Your new `index` variable will hold the position of the selected segment. Remember that indexes always start with zero. *Index 0 is 15%, index 1 is 20%, index 2 is 25%.*

Now that you have the selected segment's index, you need to determine if the first, second, or third button is selected. Then you will set the tip rate based on the selected button. This is a perfect opportunity to write an `if` statement. Before you write your `if` statement, create a variable to hold the current tip rate:

```
var tipRate: Float = 0.15
```

This line of code creates a `Float` variable named `tipRate`. You then set the default value to `0.15`. The `tipRate` variable will change based on which segment is selected. Start your `if` statement below the `tipRate` variable line:

```
var tipRate: Float = 0.15

if index == 0 {
        tipRate = 0.15
}
```

The if statement begins with the keyword `if` followed by a condition. In this case, the condition is checking whether the index's value is currently set to 0. If so, the condition will return `true`; if not, it will return `false`. If the condition is `true`, the code between the braces will execute. Otherwise the app will skip over the braces and on to the next use case. Add the following else if code to your if statement:

```
var tipRate: Float = 0.15

if index == 0 {
        tipRate = 0.15
} else if index == 1 {
        tipRate = 0.20
}
```

The else if statement checks an additional condition. If index is zero, the else if section would not execute. The else if asks if the index is 1. If this is true, it will set the tipRate variable to 0.20. Add the final section to your if statement:

```
var tipRate: Float = 0.15

if index == 0 {
        tipRate = 0.15
} else if index == 1 {
        tipRate = 0.20
} else {
        tipRate = 0.25
}
```

For the final section, you added an else statement. An else statement will be triggered for any condition that is not caught by the previous two if statements. In this case, there are only three possible answers: 0, 1, or 2. The else statement will handle the condition if the index is 2.

Now that you have the total bill and tip rate, it is time to calculate the tip. Place your cursor under the third comment line and write the following:

```
var tip: Float = totalBill * tipRate
```

This line of code creates a new Float variable named tip and sets it to the result of totalBill multiplied by tipRate. This completes step 3.

Place your cursor under the fourth comment and write this final line of code:

```
tipLabel.text = "$\(tip)"
```

This line of code sets the text attribute to your tipLabel. You created a new string using the double quotes. In the new string, you placed a dollar sign followed by the value of the tip variable. The \( ) portion of the string is used as a placeholder for any variable. In this case, the placeholder was used for the tip variable.

Click the Play button in the upper-left corner of your screen. The iOS Simulator will launch and run Tip Calculator. Click inside the Text Field and enter a value. Notice the keyboard will only allow numbers and decimal places. Next, select a tip rate and click Calculate. Your tip will be shown in the Label below.

Don't worry if you received an error, a warning, or your app did not run as expected. The best way to learn is to make mistakes. Practice makes perfect. A sample version of the project is available on AppSchool.com/book. Download it, compare it, and try, try again. Don't be afraid to start the exercise over and walk through it until you get it right.

CHAPTER 4

Diving Deeper

In this chapter, you will dive deeper into Swift. Apple provides developers with a toolset of classes and methods. This toolset, also known as a *framework*, is called *Foundation*. You can learn more about Apple's frameworks at developer.apple.com (*http://bit.ly/1xNoMn7*). However, the provided toolset is not always enough. Sometimes it is necessary to create your own class or methods. In this chapter, you will learn how to create your own classes and objects. You will also learn how to create your own methods. These skills will allow you to build a wider range of apps.

Methods

In Chapter 2, you learned about a morning routine and the list of steps you go through to get ready in the morning. Methods are a group of steps that work together to accomplish a specific task. Methods are very similar to functions. *Methods* are a set of steps to complete a task inside a class or object. A *function* is a set of steps to complete a task that stands alone. These two items are so similar, they have become synonyms. It is common to hear people use the words "method" and "function" interchangeably, even though they are usually referring to a method.

Writing your own method can be convenient for repeated work. If you were to write a method that greets you in the morning, it might look like this:

```
func goodMorning() {
    println("Good Morning")
}
```

Creating your own method starts with the func keyword. This keyword is used to declare the beginning of a new method. The next item is the method's name. Method names also use camel-casing. For example:

```
goodMorning()
```

After the method name comes a set of parentheses. Next, an open brace is used to begin the method, and a closed brace is used to end it.

Methods can take input in order to provide a more detailed decision process. For example, if you are the coach of a track and field team, it might be helpful to tell your runners how far they need to go running (i.e., "Go for a run" or "Go for a seven-mile run").

This additional input will change the final product. Input variables like these are called *parameters*. Parameters are outside values that are passed into a method. The name and type of the parameter are defined inside the parentheses. The parameters passed in will be referred to as the variable name inside the parentheses. For example:

```
func goodMorning(name: String){
        println("Good Morning \(name)")
}

//Good Morning NAME
```

Parameters are defined by first stating the variable name and then a colon followed by the type of variable. Multiple parameters can be accepted and are separated by a comma. The previous method takes a variable called name and uses it inside the welcome message:

```
func goodMorning(name: String, day: String){
        println("Good Morning \(name), Happy \(day)")
}

//Good Morning NAME-VARIABLE-HERE, happy DAY-VARIABLE-HERE
```

You can put as many lines of code inside your method as you like, but it is usually best practice to group similar lines of code into their own method and then call that method. Separating your code into small reusable methods is a great habit and will make updating your code much easier.

You created this great goodMorning method, but how do you use it? *Calling* a method is a term used to describe a line of code that triggers a method to execute. Calling a method is as simple as writing the method name followed by a set of parentheses. These empty parentheses are required, even if your method does not have any parameters. For example, consider a method named goodNight:

```
func goodNight(){
        println("Good Night")
}
```

You would execute the code inside goodNight by writing:

```
goodNight()

//"Good Night"
```

This will call the `goodNight()` method and execute the steps inside the `goodNight` method. *But what if your method takes input like goodMorning?* Consider a method that takes input parameters like this:

```
func goodMorning(name: String, day: String){
        println("Good Morning \(name), Happy \(day)")
}

//Good Morning NAME-VARIABLE-HERE, Happy DAY-VARIABLE-HERE
```

You could call the `goodMorning` method like this:

```
goodMorning("Steve",day: "Saturday")

//Good Morning Steve, Happy Saturday
```

Finally, if your method requires input and the caller forgets to provide it, you can set a default value for your parameters. If a value is not provided, the default will take its place. To set a default value to your parameter, add an equals sign next to the type and provide the default value. For example, the following code sets `"World"` and `"Day"` as the default values for the `name` and `day` parameters:

```
func goodMorning(name: String = "World", day: String = "Day"){
        println("Good Morning \(name), Happy \(day)")
}
```

Now, if a caller forgets to provide the parameters, the message is still readable:

```
goodMorning()

//Good Morning World, Happy Day
```

Return Values

Methods can do more than accept input and execute steps; they can generate output as well. When a method provides an output value, it is called a *return value*. The return value is the final product of the method, and it is sent back to the caller. A return value can be any type, but the return type must be declared by the method:

```
func sum(a: Int,b: Int) -> Int {
        return a + b
}
```

If a method provides a return value, the return type must be defined after the parameters. The *return type* is the type of variable that will be returned. To define the return type, add a dash and a greater-than sign following the parameters. The arrow, →, signifies a return value will be provided, and the type of value is stated to the right of the arrow. Finally, the `return` keyword must be used inside the method next to the variable to be returned.

No matter how many lines of code there are inside a method, the return keyword ends the method when it is executed. When the return keyword is executed, any code below the return keyword within the method will be skipped:

```
func calculateTip(bill: Float, percentage: Float)-> Float{
    var tip = bill * percentage
    return tip
}
```

Classes

Imagine you are a home builder, and you just signed a contract to build 20 similar homes in a brand new neighborhood. Before you send out the construction crew, you must first create a blueprint. A *blueprint* is a document that shows exactly how the house will look and behave. This single document is used as the template to create each of the 20 houses.

Using a blueprint or template to create objects saves time and makes maintenance much easier. This principle applies to creating virtual objects, too. The blueprints in Swift are called a *class*. A class is a blueprint or template for an object. This template can be used over and over like a printing press to create virtual objects.

A class defines the attributes and behaviors of the object. The attributes are the characteristics of the object. These attributes are defined by properties. *Properties* are variables included in each object. The properties of a house would be the exterior color, street number, and number of bathrooms.

The behaviors are the methods the object provides. For example, a method could set the air temperature to 68 degrees, or open the garage, or enable the alarm system.

Creating your own class in Swift is simple. If you wanted to create a house class for your new home building project, it would look like this:

```
class House {

}
```

The name of a class always starts with a capital letter. This allows other developers to distinguish between a class and an object. Objects and methods always start with a lowercase letter.

Properties

Adding properties to your custom class is very similar to declaring a variable. You can add some properties to your house class like this:

```
class House {
        var exteriorColor = "Brown"
        var currentAirTemp = 70
```

```
        var isGarageOpen = true
        var isAlarmEnabled = false
}
```

The class you created has four properties, each with a default value already set. This means if a new value is not provided, each house created from this house class will have a brown exterior, the garage will be open, the alarm system will be disabled, and the air temperature will be 70 degrees.

Methods

You could add some methods to the house class as well:

```
class House {
        var exteriorColor = "Brown"
        var currentAirTemp = 70
        var isGarageOpen = false
        var isAlarmEnabled = false

        func prepareForNighttime(){
                isGarageOpen = false
                isAlarmEnabled = true
                currentAirTemp = 65
        }

        func prepareForDaytime(){
                isGarageOpen = true
                isAlarmEnabled = false
                currentAirTemp = 70
        }

}
```

Notice these methods are defined just like a method. They use the same func keyword followed by the method name, parameters, and return value. Each house created with the house class will have the ability to prepare for daytime or prepare for nighttime. These methods will do things like shut the garage, enable the alarm, and adjust the air temperature.

Creating an Object

Now that you have defined the properties and methods for the house class, it is time to build your first house. To create an object from a class, you call the *initializer* method. The initializer method is a method designed specifically for setting up new objects. The initializer method is similar to walking through the setup wizard on your Mac the first time it starts up.

If you provided default values for your properties, there is no need to write an initializer method. Xcode will create one for you. The initializer method is typically accessed by writing the name of the class followed by two parentheses. For example:

```
var myHouse: House = House()
```

or:

```
var myHouse = House()
```

Either line creates a new house called myHouse.

Accessing Properties

You can access the value of a property by using dot syntax. *Dot syntax* is a format used to access and assign values to properties. Dot syntax begins with an object:

```
var myHouse = House()
```

To access the exteriorColor, write the variable name followed by a dot and then exteriorColor:

```
myHouse.exteriorColor
//Brown
```

The exeriorColor returns the string "Brown" because the property's default value is "Brown".

This simple format can be used for assigning values to properties as well. To assign a value, add an equals sign with the new value next to it:

```
myHouse.exteriorColor = "Blue"
```

This will change the exteriorColor property to "Blue":

```
myHouse.exteriorColor = "Blue"
println(myHouse.exteriorColor)

//"Blue"
```

After the code changes the exteriorColor to "Blue", the next line prints the exteriorColor of the house.

Calling Methods

You can use the methods from the house class by calling the method's name:

```
myHouse.prepareForNighttime()
```

Calling a method uses the same dot syntax you saw with properties. First, you write the name of the object and then a dot, followed by the name of the method you would like to call. Finally, the line is ended with a set of parentheses. These parentheses should include any required parameters; otherwise, they must be written and left empty.

Subclasses

When creating something, it's helpful to reuse a template instead of starting from scratch. Imagine you want to build a cabin. A cabin has many similar features to a house, but it also has a few different attributes and behaviors. Instead of drawing a completely new blueprint, you could start with the house class and then make changes from there. This process of reusing is called *subclassing*.

Subclassing provides a convenient way to share attributes and behaviors between a parent and child class. In this case, the parent class is House and the child class is Cabin. Writing a subclass is just like creating a custom class. However, the parent class name is placed after the class name and separated by a colon. For example:

```
class Cabin: House {

}
```

Inheritance

Inheritance is the ability to pass down attributes and behaviors from a parent class to a child class. All of the parent class's properties and methods will automatically be shared with the child class. For example, the cabin class inherits the properties and default values of exteriorColor, currentAirTemp, isGarageOpen, and isAlarmEnabled. The cabin class also inherits the prepareForNighttime() and prepareForDaytime() methods. However, the cabin class can add or change these if needed. For example, the cabin class may want to have "Red" as its default exteriorColor.

Overriding

But what if you don't want a brown cabin? No problem—with overriding, you can change it. Changing the inherited properties or methods in a child class is called *overriding*. Overriding allows the child class to define its own version of a particular property or method. To override a method, add the override keyword.

Overriding initializers

You can override the default value of a property using the initializer method. The initializer method is called whenever a new object is created. This means you can write your own initializer and set your own default values:

```
class House {
        var exteriorColor = "Brown"
        var currentAirTemp = 70
        var isGarageOpen = false
        var isAlarmEnabled = false

        func prepareForNighttime(){
                isGarageOpen = false
                isAlarmEnabled = true
                currentAirTemp = 65
        }

        func prepareForDaytime(){
                isGarageOpen = true
                isAlarmEnabled = false
                currentAirTemp = 70
        }

}

class Cabin: House {
        override init(){
                super.init()
                exteriorColor = "Red"
        }
}
```

The cabin class defines its own initializer method by using the init keyword. Since the cabin class overrides the initializer method from the House class, the override keyword is added to the beginning of the method name. Remember, the initializer method is automatically created for the House class. The init keyword is followed by a set of empty parentheses, and an open brace will begin the initialize method.

In the case of a subclass, the parent class's initializer should first be called before the child class overrides or makes changes. To refer to the parent class, use the super keyword. Inside the child class's init method, write **super.init()**. This will call the parent class's initializer method. Once this is complete, the child class is free to override and make changes. In this case, the cabin class sets the exteriorColor to "Red".

Overriding methods

In addition to overriding a subclass's properties, you can also override a subclass's methods. For example, when you prepare a cabin for nighttime, there are different steps required than when you prepare a house. In a house, you might shut the garage, change the central air, and arm the alarm. However, with a cabin, there is no alarm system to enable or garage to shut; you will likely just start a fire in the fireplace. To override a method, you use the override keyword:

```
class Cabin: House {
    override init(){
        super.init()
        exteriorColor = "Red"
    }

    override func prepareForNighttime(){
        startFire()
    }
}
```

In this chapter, you dove deeper into Swift. You learned how to create your own classes and methods. You also learned how to subclass and override. With these skills, you are now ready to create any class you could need to build an app. Your knowledge base is growing; now it is time to put that knowledge to work. Continue on to the Race Car exercise.

Exercise: Race Car

In this next exercise, you will create your own race car class. Your application will create a race car, tell it to honk, and then display the race car to the user. The app's user interface will look like Figure 4-1.

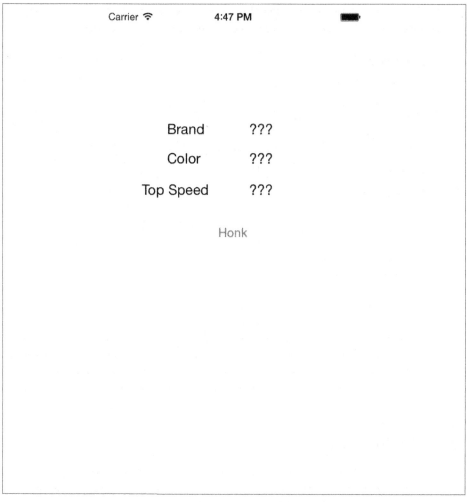

Figure 4-1. Completed Race Car exercise

Notice the interface is made up of six Labels and a Button. The application will display the properties of your new race car. The user will have the ability to honk the car as well. But, when the race car honks, no noise will be made; instead, it will write a message to the developer log.

Now that you have a set of features and a user interface, it's time to start developing the app. Open Xcode and select File→New→Project from the menu bar (Figure 4-2).

Figure 4-2. New project

Select the Single View Application template for your project (Figure 4-3).

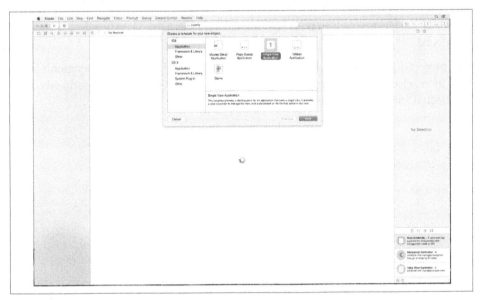

Figure 4-3. Project template dialog

Click Next and enter **RaceCar** as the Product Name (Figure 4-4).

Figure 4-4. Project detail dialog

Your Organization Name and Organization Identifier should already be completed. If they are not, enter your first and last name with no spaces. Verify the Language is set to Swift and the Devices option is set to iPhone. Leave Use Core Data unselected and then click Next.

The project directory dialog box will appear (Figure 4-5). Select your Documents folder and then select the Programming folder. Leave "Create Git Repository on My Mac" unselected and click Create.

Figure 4-5. Save project

The project details screen should start to feel familiar by now (Figure 4-6). We have the Project Navigator on the left side, the Standard Editor in the middle, and the Inspector on the right side.

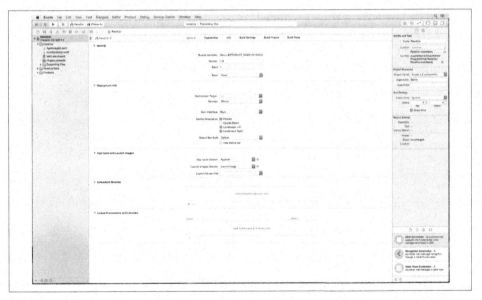

Figure 4-6. Project details

Select the *Main.storyboard* file from the Project Navigator. A blank interface will appear (Figure 4-7).

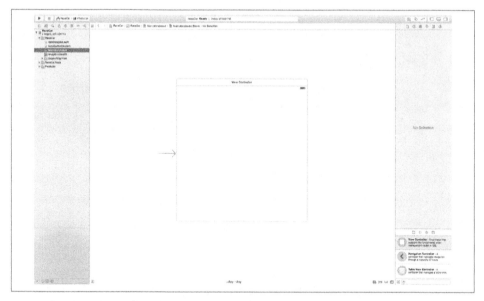

Figure 4-7. Main.storyboard

This app will run only on iPhone. Click the first tab at the top of the Inspector. The tab looks like a piece of paper with a folded corner. About halfway down, deselect the Use Auto Layout checkbox (Figure 4-8). A dialog box will appear, select iPhone, and then Disable Size Classes. The shape of the user interface will change. Auto Layout is used for multiple screen sizes and will be covered in Chapter 7 of this book.

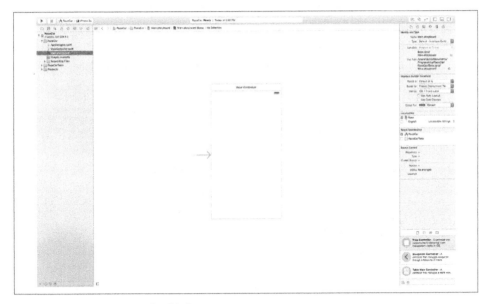

Figure 4-8. Auto Layout disabled

Check and make sure the Inspector is visible. If it is not, click the Inspector View button in the upper-right corner of your screen. The button will turn blue with a blue stripe on the right side when it is enabled (Figure 4-9).

Figure 4-9. View controls

Click the Attributes Inspector icon at the top of the Inspector. The Attributes Inspector icon is the fourth from the left and looks like a downward arrow. Finally, select the Object Library icon on the lower Inspector toolbar. The Object Library icon is the third from the left and looks like a small circle.

Once you have the Object Library open, type **Label** into the Object Library search box at the bottom of the Inspector (Figure 4-10). Click and drag three Labels onto the interface. Position the three Labels vertically on the left side of the interface (Figure 4-11).

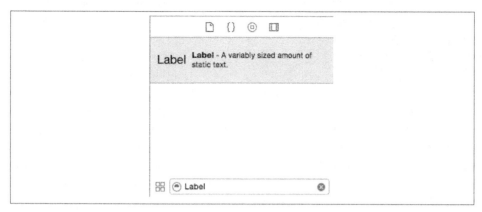

Figure 4-10. Label in Object Library

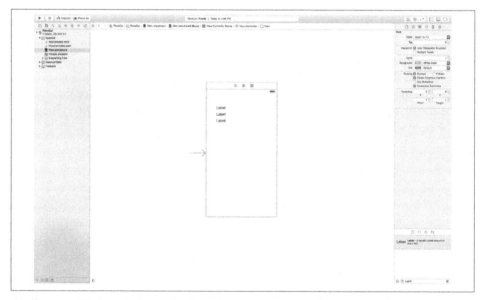

Figure 4-11. Three Labels

Once you have the three Labels aligned, click and draw a box around the Labels with your mouse.

The three Labels should now all be selected (Figure 4-12). You can tell that the Labels are selected because each Label will have small white boxes surrounding it. Next, go to the top menu bar and select Edit→Copy or press Command+C (Figure 4-13).

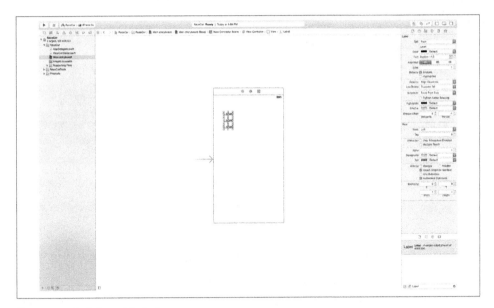

Figure 4-12. Selected Labels

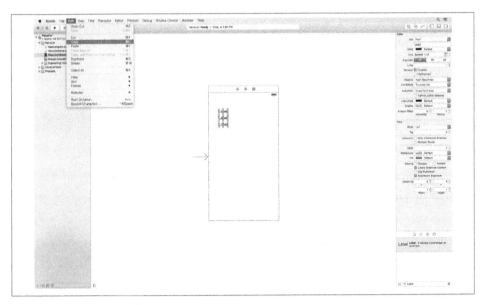

Figure 4-13. Copy Labels

Then go to the top menu bar and select Edit→Paste or press Command+V (Figure 4-14).

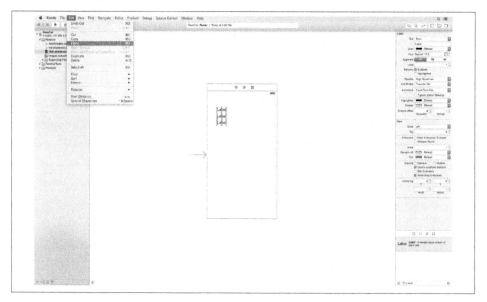

Figure 4-14. Paste Labels

The three new Labels will be added to the interface. These new Labels will all be selected. Click the topmost new Label and drag it to the right side of the interface. The other two new Labels will follow the Label you dragged across. Ensure that each Label is lined up with a Label on the other side (Figure 4-15).

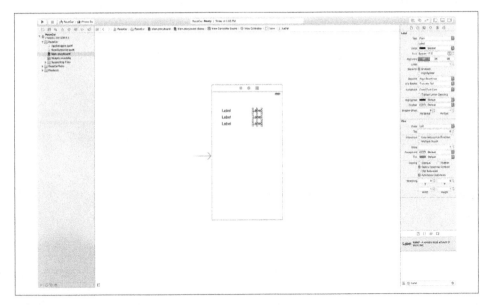

Figure 4-15. New Labels

Copy and pasting elements on the interface is sometimes more convenient than drag-
ging six Labels from the Object Library. Finally, erase the Label text inside the Object
Library search box and type **Button** (Figure 4-16).

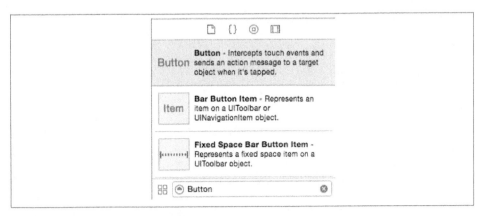

Figure 4-16. Button in Object Library

Drag a Button from the Object Library and position it in the center just below the Labels
(Figure 4-17).

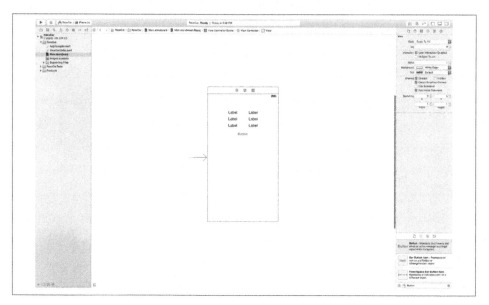

Figure 4-17. New Button

Double-click the Label in the upper-left corner of the interface. Replace the text with **Brand** (Figure 4-18). Double-click and change the middle Label on the left side to **Color**. Finally, double-click and change the bottom left Label to **Top Speed**. Realign the Labels as needed.

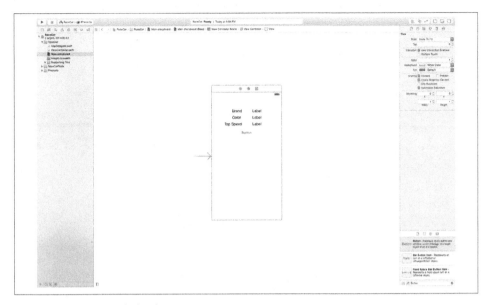

Figure 4-18. New Label titles

The Labels on the left will serve as descriptors for the Labels on the right. The value for each attribute of your race car will be displayed in the Labels on the right, as in Table 4-1.

Table 4-1. Race car

Brand	Ferrari
Color	Red
Top speed	200 mph

Double-click each Label on the right side and set the text to **????** (Figure 4-19). Then drag the upper-right corner of each right-side label until the width is at least 60 pts.

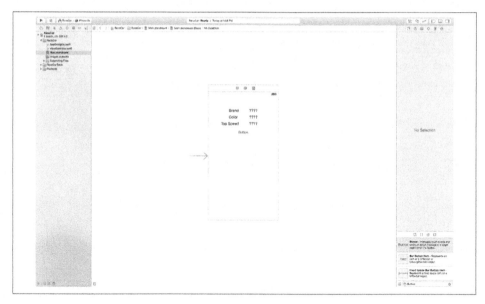

Figure 4-19. More new titles

Finally, double-click the Button and set the text to **Honk**. Then drag the upper-right corner of the Button until the width is at least 60 pts (Figure 4-20).

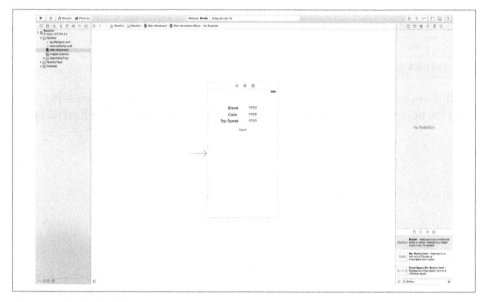

Figure 4-20. Resized Button

Now that your interface is complete, it is time to connect the view to the controller. In this case, the controller is *ViewController.swift* file. In the upper-right corner of the screen, click the Assistant Editor button. This will open the Assistant Editor on the right side of your screen (Figure 4-21).

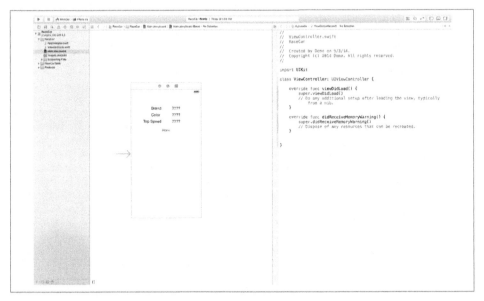

Figure 4-21. Assistant Editor

To clean up more space, hide the Inspector by clicking the Inspector View button in the upper-right corner of your screen.

The Assistant Editor will open the *ViewController.swift* file automatically. You can verify this by checking the current file shown at the top of the Assistant Editor, right next to the word "Automatic."

Not all of the elements on the interface need to be connected to the controller. There is no reason to connect an element that is static or will not change. The three Labels on the left side of the interface will not change throughout the lifetime of this app. This means you can safely leave these Labels disconnected from the controller.

Select the upper-right Label on the interface. While holding the Control key, click and drag from the Label to just below the following words:

```
class ViewController: UIViewController {
```

Release your mouse when you see a blue horizontal line (Figure 4-22); the connection dialog will be shown (Figure 4-23).

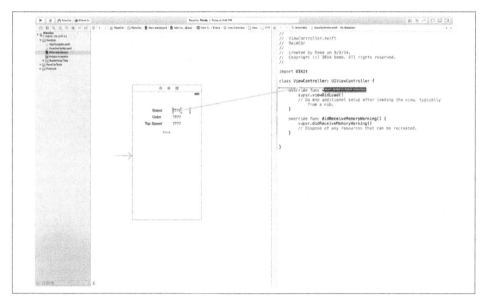

Figure 4-22. Control-drag connection

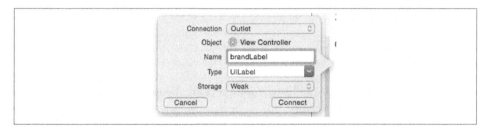

Figure 4-23. Pop-up connection dialog

Since the element is a Label, the connection is automatically set to Outlet. Enter **brand Label** for the name. Click Connect when finished.

Code was generated for you when you clicked the Connect button. Take a look at the code written by Xcode:

```
@IBOutlet var brandLabel : UILabel!
```

The first keyword @IBOutlet is used to declare an outlet connection between the views. You know the var keyword is used to declare a variable. brandLabel is the name of your new variable, the colon is used to designate the type of variable, and the UILabel is the type. The new brandLabel variable will be used to reference the upper-right Label on the interface.

Select the middle Label on the right side of the interface. While holding the Control key, click and drag from the Label to just below the following words:

```
class ViewController: UIViewController {
```

Be careful not to release your mouse while hovering over the generated code from the brandLabel. A light blue box will appear if you incorrectly hover over another Label's code. This can cause confusing issues. Be sure to only release your mouse when you see a dark blue horizontal line (Figure 4-24). If done correctly, the connection dialog will be shown (Figure 4-25).

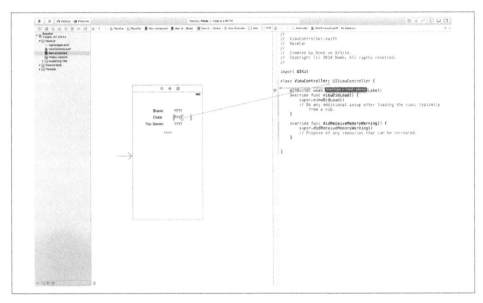

Figure 4-24. Control-drag connection

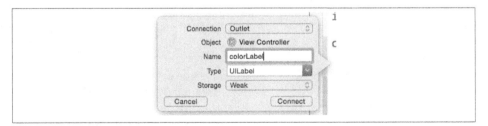

Figure 4-25. Pop-up connection dialog

Since the element is a Label, the connection is automatically set to Outlet. Enter **color Label** for the name. Click Connect when finished.

More code was generated for you when you clicked the Connect button.

Select the bottom-right Label on the right side of the interface. While holding the Control key, click and drag from the Label to just below the following words:

```
class ViewController: UIViewController {
```

Be sure to only release your mouse when you see a dark blue horizontal line (Figure 4-26); the connection dialog will be shown (Figure 4-27).

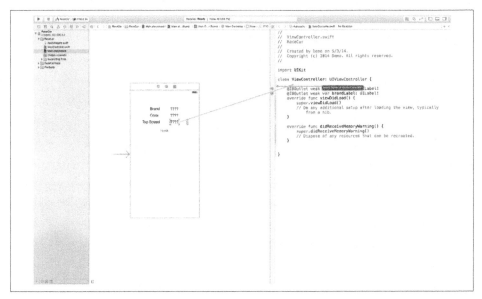

Figure 4-26. Control-drag connection

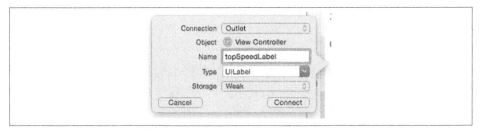

Figure 4-27. Pop-up connection dialog

Since the element is a Label, the connection is automatically set to Outlet. Enter **top SpeedLabel** for the variable name. Notice the use of camel-casing. Click Connect when finished.

More code was generated for you when you clicked the Connect button.

Finally, you must connect the Button to the controller. A Button triggers an event inside the controller when the user taps it. This view to the controller connection pattern is called an *action*.

Select the Button in the middle of the interface. While holding the Control key, click and drag from the Label to just below the following words:

```
class ViewController: UIViewController {
```

Be sure to only release your mouse when you see a blue horizontal line (Figure 4-28); the connection dialog will be shown (Figure 4-29).

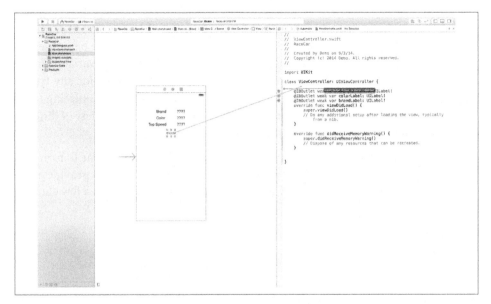

Figure 4-28. Control-drag connection

Figure 4-29. Pop-up connection dialog

Since the element is a Button, the connection must be set to action. Click the drop-down box next to Connection and select Action. Enter **honkTapped** for the action name. Leave the rest of the options alone and click Connect.

Look at the generated code created for the honkTapped action. Actions generate methods, while outlets generate variables. The method honkTapped will be called each time the Button is tapped. Take a look at the code generated by Xcode:

```
@IBAction func honkTapped(sender : AnyObject) {

}
```

The @IBAction keyword is used to declare the connection as an action. The func keyword is used to declare a method. The honkTapped portion will be used to call or execute the method. The parentheses declare the parameter or input. Inside the parentheses is the variable name for the parameter followed by a colon and the type of variable. In this case, you see the type AnyObject. AnyObject is used as a placeholder for any type of object. The sender parameter created by Xcode will provide a variable pointing to the element that triggered the action. This sender parameter could be a variety of different types like a Button, a Slider, or a Segmented Control.

The user interface has been fully connected to the controller. It's now time to turn your attention to building your very own race car. However, Apple does not provide a race car class. No problem, you can build your own custom classes with just a few clicks.

Select File→New→File (Figure 4-30).

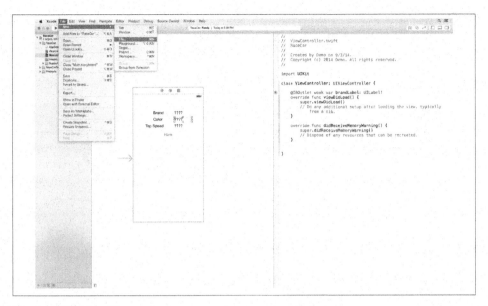

Figure 4-30. New file

Then select Cocoa Touch Class (Figure 4-31).

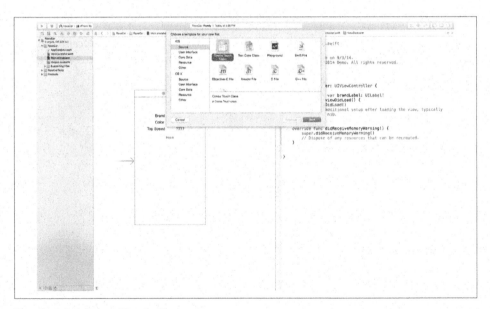

Figure 4-31. Cocoa Touch Class

Enter **RaceCar** in the Class field (Figure 4-32). Set the "Subclass of:" field to NSObject. Finally, make sure Language is set to Swift. Click Next.

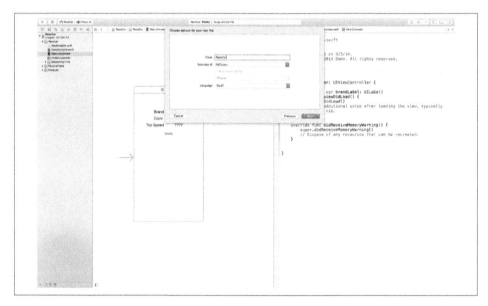

Figure 4-32. Name class

Xcode will now ask you where you would like to save your files. The *RaceCar* project directory should already be selected. If not, select the *RaceCar* directory inside of */Documents/Programming/RaceCar* and then click Create (Figure 4-33).

Figure 4-33. Save class

You will notice a new file selected, *RaceCar.swift*, in the Project Navigator. The new RaceCar class file will also be open inside the Editor (Figure 4-34).

Figure 4-34. New RaceCar.swift file

Your RaceCar will have three properties and one method. Each RaceCar will have the following properties: brand, color, and top speed. Moreover, your RaceCar will be able to honk. When your RaceCar honks, the app will not make a noise, but instead write a message to the developer log. The developer log is a great tool to keep track of variables and events while an app is running. Users cannot see the developer log. The developer log is also a great tool to triage issues or crashes.

Create your first property for the RaceCar class:

```
class RaceCar: NSObject {
        var brand: String = "Ferrari"
}
```

Adding a property is very similar to creating a variable. However, a property can be accessed by other objects. The var keyword is used to create the property. The property name comes after the var keyword. Next, there is a colon followed by the variable type. Finally, you set the variable equal to a default value with an equals sign and a string inside double quotes.

Add the next property to the RaceCar class:

```
class RaceCar: NSObject{
        var brand: String = "Ferrari"
        var color: String = "Red"
}
```

Add the color property with the same syntax and format used for the brand property. The property name is color, and the default value will be "Red". The name of the color will be stored using a String variable.

Finally, add the topSpeed property to the RaceCar class:

```
class RaceCar: NSObject{
        var brand: String = "Ferrari"
        var color: String = "Red"
        var topSpeed: Int = 200
}
```

The topSpeed property uses the same syntax but has a few different values. The type is set to Int, because it will store the top speed of the car as a whole number. Also, set the default value to **200**; quotes are not used with integer values.

The properties of the RaceCar class are now complete. This means each RaceCar created will have a brand, color, and top speed. The default values for each will be set to "Ferrari", "Red", and 200.

The RaceCar objects should also honk. This behavior will be defined as a method. Add the honk method to the RaceCar class:

```
class RaceCar: NSObject{
        var brand: String = "Ferrari"
        var color: String = "Red"
        var topSpeed: Int = 200

        func honk(){
                println("Honk! Honk!")
        }
}
```

The func keyword is used to declare the method. The honk keyword is used as the method's name. Finally, the empty parentheses state there will not be any input or parameters for the method.

Inside the method, between the open and closed braces, is only one line of code. The println keyword will take a String parameter and write the string to the developer log. Parentheses surround the String parameter, in this case, "Honk! Honk!". When this line of code is executed, Xcode will present the message in the Debug Console.

The Debug Console, or *Debugger*, is typically hidden while writing code and shown when the app is running (Figure 4-35). To show the Debugger, look at the view buttons in the upper-right corner of the screen. The middle button with the dark stripe across the bottom will show and hide the Debugger.

Figure 4-35. Debugger

The RaceCar class is complete. It's now time to create a race car using the RaceCar class. Save the RaceCar class by pressing Command+S on your keyboard.

Open the *ViewController.swift* file by clicking on it in the Project Navigator. Hide the Assistant Editor by clicking the Standard Editor button in the upper-right corner. The Standard Editor button has a few lines and is the first from the left.

Place your cursor inside the honkTapped method and add the following code:

```
@IBAction func honkTapped(sender: AnyObject) {
        //Create Car
        //Display Car
        //Honk Car
    }
```

Place the cursor under the //Create Car line and type the following:

```
var myCar = RaceCar()
```

The var keyword is used to create a variable; myCar is the variable name of your new RaceCar. The equals sign is used to set the variable to the value on the right. Finally, a new RaceCar is created with RaceCar().

RaceCar() calls the RaceCar initialize method and returns a new RaceCar with default values. The initialize method was generated by Xcode. To create an object from a class, write the class name followed by a set of parentheses. In this case, there are no required parameters, so the parentheses are empty.

Now there is a new RaceCar set to the myCar variable. Place your cursor under the //Display Car comment and write the following:

```
brandLabel.text = myCar.brand
```

This line sets the brand label on the interface to the car's brand; in this case, "Ferrari". brandLabel is the variable that represents the brand label on the interface. The dot provides access to the properties and methods of the Label. In this case, the dot is followed by the text property. The equals sign assigns myCar's brand to brandLabel's text property.

The myCar variable represents the new RaceCar you created. The dot provides access to the properties and methods of the RaceCar. The brand property is accessed by writing the word brand. This returns a string and the brandLabel's text property takes a string as input.

Add the following code to the //Display Car section:

```
colorLabel.text = myCar.color
topSpeedLabel.text = "\(myCar.topSpeed)"
```

You will notice the colorLabel line is very similar to the brandLabel line. The colorLabel line takes the color of the RaceCar and assigns it to the color label on the interface. In this case, the color assigned is the default value, "Red".

The `topSpeedLabel` line is a little different from the first two. The `topSpeedLabel` should be set to the RaceCar's `topSpeed` value. Labels require a `String` variable for their text property. However, a RaceCar's `topSpeed` is stored as an integer, not a string. This problem is easily solved with string interpolation.

Place the cursor under the `//Honk Car` line and add the following:

```
myCar.honk()
```

This line will trigger the honk method for the `RaceCar`. The honk method will write a message to the Debugger. `myCar` is the `RaceCar` object. The dot provides access to the properties and methods. Finally, the honk method is called with `honk()`. The empty parentheses are added because there are no parameters for this method.

Now it is time to see the app in action. Click the Play button in the upper-left corner of the screen. Xcode will build the code into an app and launch the iOS Simulator (Figure 4-36).

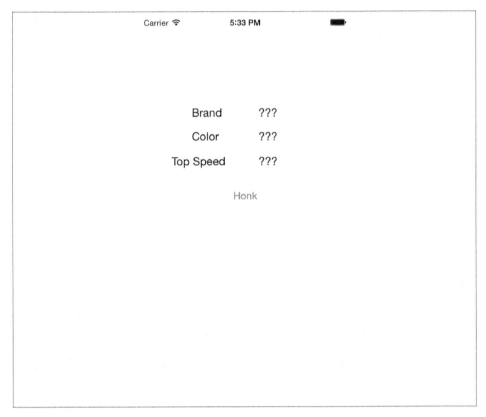

Figure 4-36. RaceCar running

Once the app has launched, click the Honk button (Figure 4-37).

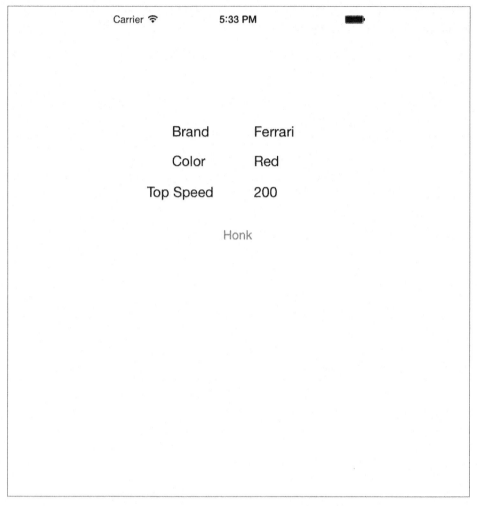

Figure 4-37. RaceCar complete

The app creates a RaceCar and displays the RaceCar's properties in the Labels. The app also calls the RaceCar's honk() method and writes a message to the Debugger. Look toward the bottom-right corner of your screen, and you should see the Debugger. If not, click the middle view button in the upper-right corner of the screen. The Debugger will show the message "Honk! Honk!".

Don't worry if you received an error, a warning, or your app did not run as expected. The best way to learn is to make mistakes. Practice makes perfect. A sample version of the project is available on AppSchool.com/book. Download it, compare it, and try, try again. Don't be afraid to start the exercise over and walk through it until you get it right.

CHAPTER 5

Building Multiscreen Apps

In this chapter, you will learn how to manage multiple screens inside one app. You will also learn how to make a scrolling list of items. Most apps have multiple screens and at least one scrolling list. This chapter will build on your knowledge base and bring you closer to releasing an app to the App Store.

View Controllers

View controllers are the logic portion of the *Model-View-Controller*, or MVC, paradigm. See Chapter 1 for a quick review of MVC. It won't surprise you to learn that a view controller is a controller that controls the view. Don't overthink it. The view displays information and receives input from the user, but it does not make decisions. Those decisions are made inside the view controller.

UIViewController

Apple highly encourages the MVC approach to development. They recommend it so much that they created their own controller called the `UIViewController`. `UIView Controller` is part of UIKit. UIKit is a set of classes provided to create interface elements. You will see the prefix UI before any class that is part of UIKit.

`UIViewController` has been configured to handle much of the heavy lifting for you. It comes with a `view` property out of the box. The `view` property is connected to a view file, in most cases, a storyboard file.

`UIViewController` also has prewritten methods ready for you. Common events like the view loading on the screen or the view disappearing from the screen are already written for you. These methods can be filled with your own custom code.

Overall, `UIViewController` provides methods and properties you would have needed to write anyway. This makes `UIViewController` a perfect parent class to use as a template for your own custom class.

For example, it is common to subclass `UIViewController` and add some code to run when the view is first loaded on to the screen. This is handled in `viewDidLoad`:

```
class mySubController: UIViewController{
    override func viewDidLoad() {
        super.viewDidLoad()
        // Do any addition setup after loading the view
    }
}
```

Take a look at the `viewDidLoad()` method inside of the `mySubController` class. The `override` keyword is used to tell Xcode that you would like to add to or change `UIView Controller`'s default `viewDidLoad` method. The `func` keyword declares the method. The term `viewDidLoad` is the method name you would like to override from `UIView Controller`. The `viewDidLoad` method does not take any parameters, so the parentheses are left blank. Finally, you add a set of open and closed braces. These braces are used to determine the beginning and end of the method.

Whenever you are overriding a method, the first line of code should make a call to `super`. `super` is a keyword used to reference the parent class of the current class. In this case, the parent class is `UIViewController`. This call to `super` is important because without it the `viewDidLoad()` method call would do absolutely nothing before your code was executed, just like if you were going to build a house but did not first lay the foundation. In this case, a call to `super.viewDidLoad()` sets the foundation. Then you can add your own custom code after the foundation is complete:

```
class mySubController: UIViewController{
    override func viewDidLoad() {
        super.viewDidLoad()

        // Do any addition setup after loading the view
        println("The View Has Loaded")
    }
}
```

The `println` method call will print the message "The View Has Loaded" to the Debugger when `viewDidLoad` executes. It's a good habit to remember each `UIViewController` in your app will have a dedicated view and controller.

UINavigationController

Up until now, each of the apps you created has only one view. However, many of the most popular apps on iOS use multiple views and transition from left to right. For example, the Mail app will slide a new view onto the screen when you tap an email. The

Mail app also provides a back button to go back as well. This left-to-right or transition behavior is created by a navigation controller.

A `UINavigationController` can hold many `UIViewControllers` in an array. Remember, an array is a collection type; it holds many items in a specific order. The navigation controller uses a sorting mechanism called a *stack*. A stack sorts items in a first-in, last-out order. A stack is similar to boarding an airplane. If you are first to board the plane you go to the very back and then when it is time to leave you are the last to get out. This is a first-in, last-out sorting paradigm at work.

Imagine you are the first to board a plane. You walk to the very back and take the window seat. Then a male passenger boards and takes the middle seat next to you. Then a female passenger boards and takes the aisle seat. When it comes time to exit the plane, the female passenger must exit first. Then the male passenger exits, and then finally you can exit the plane. A stack loads and unloads in reverse order. It loads from bottom to top and then unloads from top to bottom.

To add a view controller to the navigation controller, you *push* the view controller on top of the navigation controller. A push is equivalent to the first person boarding an airplane. The item goes as far toward the bottom as possible, but does not pass the items inserted before it. The topmost view controller in the stack will be displayed to the user. To show another view controller on top of the current one, push on the new view controller.

To remove the current view from the display, a *pop* is executed on the navigation controller. A pop removes the topmost item from the stack. In this case, it removes the current view and displays the previous view. A pop is equivalent to the first-class passengers leaving the plane: last in, first out.

When a view is displayed inside of a navigation controller, a navigation bar is added to the top of the current view. This navigation bar has three main sections: the left `UIBar ButtonItem`, the `titleView`, and the right `UIBarButtonItem`. A `UIBarButtonItem` acts like a typical button, but it lives inside a `UINavigationBar`. `UINavigationBar` is the class used to create the navigation bar at the top of a navigation controller. The `leftBarBut tonItem` will automatically become a back button when another view is shown in the navigation controller. The `titleView` will display the value from the `UIView Controller`'s `title` property. The key to remember here is that the title is defined by the view controller, but shown by the navigation controller. Setting the `title` to a view controller is simple:

```
title = "Countries"
```

Each view controller has a `title` property, because `UIViewController` defines the `title` property. The back button will also use the *title* from the previous view controller instead of the word "Back."

Finally, the right `UIBarButtonItem` is optional; this is a location where a primary or secondary action could be placed. For example, a settings button could be placed in the upper-right corner.

Table View

A scrolling list of items is one of the most common interfaces used in iOS Apps. For example, the Settings app has a scrolling list of categories and when the user taps on an item, another screen with more details is shown. This effect is achieved by the combination of a navigation controller and table views. The navigation controller controls which view is currently displayed, and the table view displays the scrolling list of items.

Table views are made up of a few key parts. Each item or row in the list is called a *cell*. A cell is a view used to display an individual row in the table view. The table view has many cells, and they are grouped into sections. Sections are used to separate rows into groups. The Settings app uses sections to group categories like Notification Center, Control Center, and Do Not Disturb. Each table view has a header and footer. The header is a view that sits above the cells, while the footer sits at the bottom after the cells.

Finally, a table view is set to one of two styles. The default style, Plain, lists each row one after another with no separation. The other style, Grouped, will separate rows by their section and place a divider between each group.

Delegation

Most sports websites and apps provide a service that sends alerts to your phone or email whenever your favorite team scores. For example, you might receive a buzz on your phone whenever a San Francisco Giants player hits a home run. These updates are only shown when a particular event happens, and the event could happen at any time. Since there is no scheduled time for these events, an update is sent to the subscriber whenever the event occurs.

This same notification concept is used to alert a controller when an event has happened inside the app. The process of subscribing to or receiving notifications for a particular event is called *delegation*. Delegation specifies a delegate to receive all notifications. However, the delegate doesn't just receive the notifications; in most cases, the delegate must respond to them as well.

For example, if you are the manager of a company, you might tell your security officer to monitor the break room and knock on your door whenever there are more than three people in the break room at a time. The knock would serve as a notification, and you could choose how you would like to handle the notification each time you are notified.

When a table view is first being created, there are a series of questions that must be answered. The table view sets a delegate to receive the questions and provide answers.

For example, the table view will ask the delegate how many rows should be created. The delegate could respond with a specific number like 20 or even an integer variable.

Instead of answering questions, you override a specific method for each piece of information. For example, to provide the number of rows, you override the `numberOfRows InSection` method:

```
override func tableView(tableView: UITableView,
        numberOfRowsInSection section: Int) -> Int {

        //Return the number of rows in the section
        return 10
}
```

Don't worry about understanding every part of this method; just focus on the code inside the method. In this case, the `numberOfRowsInSection` method returns an integer. Set the return to 10, and 10 rows will be created inside the table view. This is just one of many questions that must be answered to create a table view.

The full list of questions are wrapped up inside a protocol. A *protocol* is a specific way of doing something. For example, the protocol at the airport is to check your baggage, go through security, and then board the plane. During each of these steps, you may be asked to provide some input like your destination. The key is that you must agree to complete all the required steps in the protocol. In development, this is called *conforming*. Conforming is agreeing that you will respond to all of the required methods in a protocol.

UITableViewController

`UIViewController` is a view controller class created by Apple to help set up the typical methods and properties most view controllers need. In the same light, `UITableView Controller` handles the heavy lifting for creating a view controller with a table view. `UITableViewController` will automatically create a table view and set it to a property named `tableView`. It will also specify itself as the delegate and stub out all of the required delegate methods. A *stubbed-out method* is a term used to describe a method that is declared with nothing inside of it yet. Finally, the `UITableViewController` will take care of highlighting and unhighlighting rows when they are tapped. It makes creating and managing table views a breeze.

UITableViewDataSource

The delegate protocol that holds the three required methods for `UITableView` is called `UITableViewDataSource`. This protocol gathers information for the number of sections, the number of rows in each section, and the cells to be displayed.

The first required method is numberOfSectionsInTableView(_:). This method asks for an integer representing the number of sections in the table view. Overriding this method is straightforward. For example, the method will look like this inside the UITableViewController:

```
override func numberOfSectionsInTableView(tableView: UITableView) -> Int {
    //#warning Potentially incomplete method implementation.
    //return the number of sections.
    return 0
}
```

Notice the return line is currently set to 0; this means there will be zero sections in the table view. Apple has added a warning comment to remind you to override this method. If there are zero sections, then no rows will be shown. It is important to remember that sections hold cells; without a section, no cells will be shown:

```
override func numberOfSectionsInTableView(tableView: UITableView) -> Int {

    //return the number of sections.
    return 1
}
```

The next required method is tableView(_:numberOfRowsInSection:). This method asks for an integer representing the total number of rows for a given section:

```
override func tableView(tableView: UITableView,
  numberOfRowsInSection section: Int) -> Int {

    //#warning Incomplete method implementation
    // Return the number of rows in the section

    return 0
}
```

Notice the return line is currently set to 0; this means there will be zero rows in each section of the table view. Apple has added a warning to remind you to override this method:

```
override func tableView(tableView: UITableView,
  numberOfRowsInSection section: Int) -> Int {
    //#warning Incomplete method implementation
    // Return the number of rows in the section

    return 5
}
```

Finally, the UITableViewDataSource protocol requires that you respond to table View(:cellForRowAtIndexPath:). This method provides the cell for each row in the table view. The method provides a parameter named indexPath. The indexPath parameter is an NSIndexPath. NSIndexPath has two properties. The section property is the index of the current section. The row property is the index of the current row. *Remember counting starts at 0 with all indexes.* This means:

- The first row in the first section would have an NSIndexPath of 0,0.
- The fourth row in the first section would have an NSIndexPath of 0,3.
- The first row in the third section would have an NSIndexPath of 2,0.

The row and section property are available via dot notation. For example:

```
var currentRow = indexPath.row
var currentSection = indexPath.section
```

The tableView(:cellForRowAtIndexPath:) can be daunting, but do not be worried, because it will all make sense after a little while. Take a look at the method provided by UITableViewController. Just focus on the inside of the method for now. Remember, don't be afraid to make mistakes:

```
override func tableView(tableView: UITableView,
cellForRowAtIndexPath indexPath: NSIndexPath) -> UITableViewCell {

        let cell =
        tableView.dequeueReusableCellWithIdentifier
        ("Cell", forIndexPath: indexPath) as UITableViewCell

        return cell
}
```

Cell reuse

The first line creates a constant named cell. cell is set equal to one of the table view's dequeued cells. A *dequeued* cell is a cell that is no longer being used. Just like the real world, it's important to recycle resources if possible. When there is a table view with more rows than the display can show, the other rows are not actually created. Instead, when a row rolls off the top or bottom of the display, it is placed in a recycling bin. Then before another cell is created, the recycling bin is checked to see if a recycled cell is available. Because cells can be reused, it is important to clear their contents before re-using them.

The table view is accessed by using the tableView variable. Then the dequeueReusa bleCellWithIdentifier method will grab a recycled cell or create a new one if needed. The dequeueReusableCellWithIdentifier method accepts two parameters: identi fier, a String to classify a special type of cell, and forIndexPath, an NSIndexPath specifying the location.

The cellForRowAtIndexPath method starts with the override keyword, because this method was inherited from UITableViewController. The cellForRowAtIndexPath method will be customized outside of its original behavior. The func keyword is used to declare the method. The first `tableView` is part of the method name. The parentheses hold the parameters for the method. The first parameter is named `tableView` and is a `UITableView`. The `cellForRowAtIndexPath` is the method name. The next parameter is an `NSIndexPath` named `indexPath`. Finally, the method will return a `UITableViewCell`.

Once you have a cell, you can set the properties of the cell to display your data.

There are five main properties to each `UITableViewCell`:

`textLabel`
UILabel displays the main message text.

`detailTextLabel`
UILabel displays a subtitle; this label is not always shown.

`imageView`
UIImageView displays UIImage on the left side of the cell.

`accessoryView`
Displays disclosure icons if applicable.

`contentView`
UIView, blank canvas that holds all the elements.

`UITableViewCells` have four different styles; depending on the style, each of the five properties may be positioned differently or hidden completely:

Default
Left-aligned text label, optional `imageView`, and no `detailTextLabel`.

Value1
Left-side label with black text; it also has a right-side label that has smaller blue text and is right-aligned.

Value2
Left-side label that is right-aligned and contains blue text; on the right side is a left-aligned label with black text.

Subtitle
Left-side left-aligned label with black text; it also has a lower left-side left-aligned label with smaller gray text.

In this chapter, you learned how to manage multiple screens inside one app. You also learned how to make a scrolling list of items. Your knowledge base is growing. Now it is time to put your knowledge to the test. Keep up the momentum and get started on the Passport exercise.

Exercise: Passport

The exercise in this chapter is called Passport. Passport is a simple application that displays a person's name, birthday, nationality, and photo (Figure 5-1). Passport will also show a list of countries to which you have traveled. This project will be used in future chapters; be sure to follow along closely.

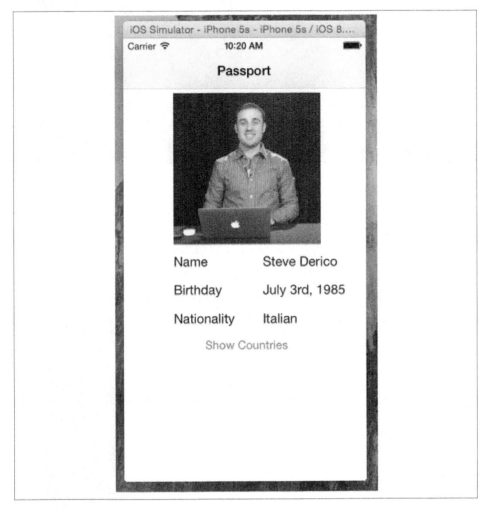

Figure 5-1. Passport app

Open Xcode from your Dock and select File→New→Project (Figure 5-2).

Figure 5-2. New project

Select Single View Application and click Next (Figure 5-3).

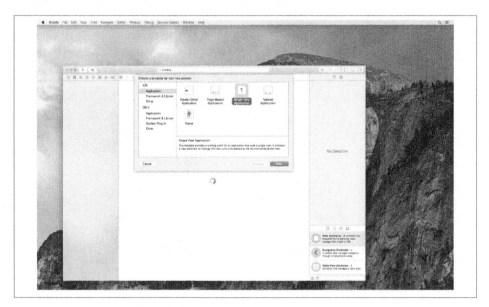

Figure 5-3. Project template dialog

Name the product **Passport**, verify the language is set to Swift, and set the Devices drop-down menu to iPhone (Figure 5-4). Click Next.

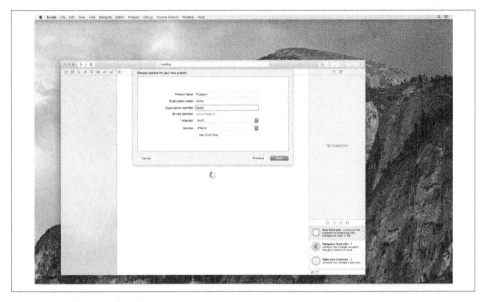

Figure 5-4. Project details

Save the project inside the Programming folder (Figure 5-5).

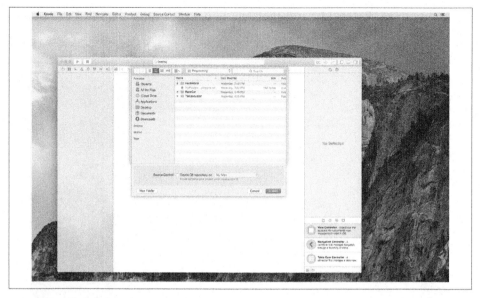

Figure 5-5. Save project

The project details will be displayed (Figure 5-6). Deselect the Landscape Left and Landscape Right orientations. Then open *Main.storyboard* (Figure 5-7).

Figure 5-6. Project details

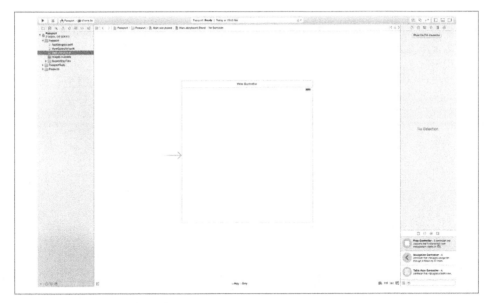

Figure 5-7. Main.storyboard

Look at the Inspector on the right side of your screen. Show the File Inspector by clicking on the first icon in the upper toolbar. The icon looks like a small piece of paper with its corner bent.

Scroll down to the Interface Builder Document section and deselect Use Auto Layout (Figures 5-8 and 5-9). A dialog box will appear; select iPhone and then Disable Size Classes.

Figure 5-8. Disable Auto Layout

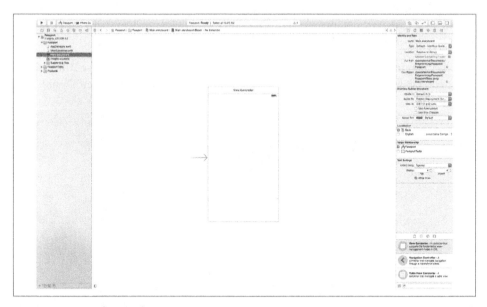

Figure 5-9. Interface without Auto Layout

Select the interface, then from the top menu bar select Editor→Embed In→Navigation Controller.

A new scene will be added to the Storyboard, *Navigation Controller Scene* (Figure 5-10). A *scene* represents another screen or interface inside your app. The Navigation Controller Scene is connected to the original View Controller Scene. This connection declares the View Controller Scene will be the first view controller shown inside the navigation controller. Then open the Document Outline by clicking the small box in the bottom left of the Storyboard Editor. The Document Outline shows a hierarchy of all the elements in the storyboard file. Then hide the Project Navigator (Figure 5-11).

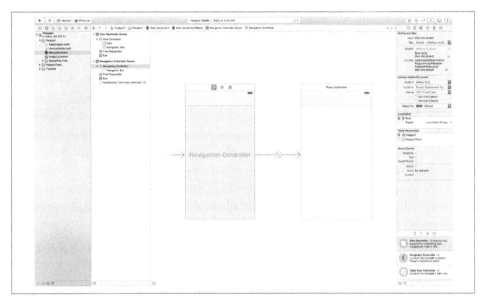

Figure 5-10. New navigation controller

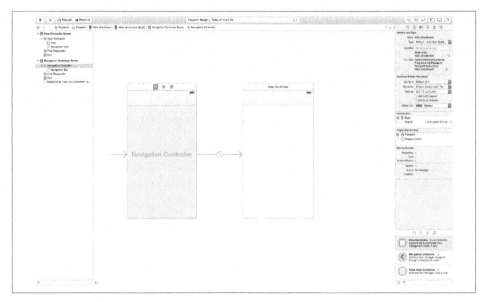

Figure 5-11. Hide Project Navigator

At the top of the View Controller Scene is a light gray box; this is the navigation bar. Double-click it, type **Passport**, and then press Return.

In the bottom half of the Inspector, click the Object Library search box and type **Image View** (Figure 5-12).

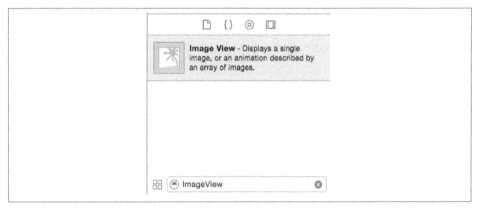

Figure 5-12. Image View in Object Library

Drag an Image View onto the top half of the view controller's view. Then open the Size Inspector; its icon looks like a ruler, and it is the second from the right (Figure 5-13).

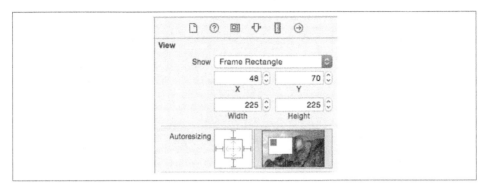

Figure 5-13. Size Inspector

Enter **48** for X, **70** for Y, **225** for Width, and **225** for Height. Then deselect the two crossing arrows inside the Autoresizing box (Figure 5-14).

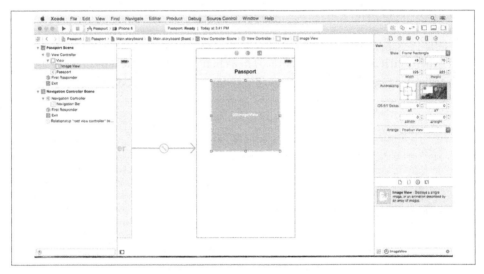

Figure 5-14. Repositioned Image View

Drag out a Label and position it under the Image View's bottom-left corner. Place two more Labels under this Label. Select all three Labels and open the Attributes Inspector. The Attributes Inspector is the fourth icon from the left. Next to the font input box is a small box with a *T* inside it. Click this box, and a pop-up menu will appear. Click the font drop-down menu and change it to System Bold (Figure 5-15). Click Done.

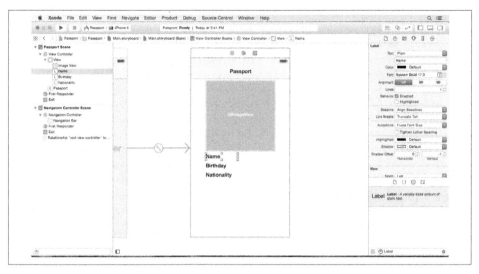

Figure 5-15. Bold font

The left-side labels will now be truncated; drag the sizing handle on the right side of each Label until it is at least 100 pts wide. Then change the Labels' text by double-clicking each Label. Change the Labels to `Name`, `Birthday`, and `Nationality` (Figure 5-16).

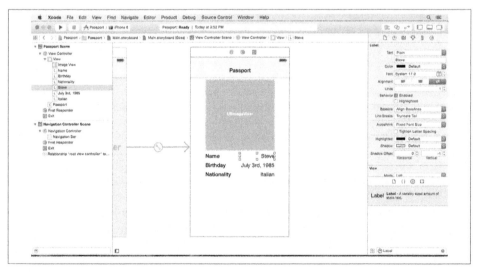

Figure 5-16. Right-side Labels

Then drag out three more Labels and place them in the bottom-right corner of the Image View. These right-side Labels should align with the left-side Labels. Then select all the right-side Labels and open the Attributes Inspector. Next to the Alignment property, click the third button. This will right-align the text inside the Labels. Drag the left-sizing handle for each new Label until they are all at least 100 pts wide. Change the right-side labels to match your name, birthday, and nationality.

Download an image of yourself from the Web. Next select File→Add Files to Passport (Figure 5-17). Browse to a photo of yourself. Verify that "Copy Items if needed" is selected, select the image file, and click Add. Select the Image View and then click the Image drop-down in the Attributes Inspector. Select the newly added photo (Figure 5-18).

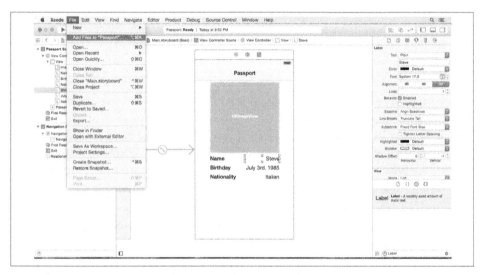

Figure 5-17. Add file to Passport

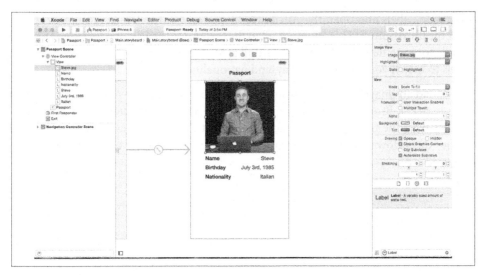

Figure 5-18. Newly added image

The photo may look stretched or skewed. To fix this, click the Mode drop-down menu inside the Attributes Inspector. Then select Aspect Fill; this will ensure that the aspect ratio of the image is not changed, and the image will fill the inside of the Image View. Experiment with the other modes to see what works best.

Drag a Button from the Object Library and position it under the personal details. Double-click the button and name it **Show Countries** (Figure 5-19). When tapped, this button should show a list of visited countries.

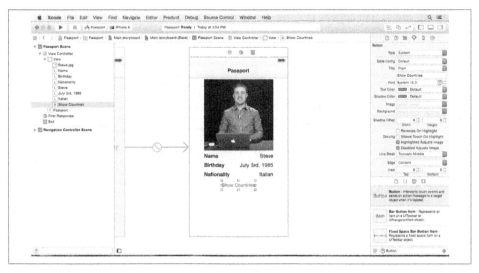

Figure 5-19. Show Countries button

A list of countries will be shown when the user taps the Show Countries button. Lists are best handled by table views. Apple has provided a controller designed especially for working with table views, called `UITableViewController`. Drag a Table View Controller out from the Object Library. Place it to the right of the Passport Scene.

Next, select the Show Countries button and Control-drag from the button to the table view controller (Figure 5-20).

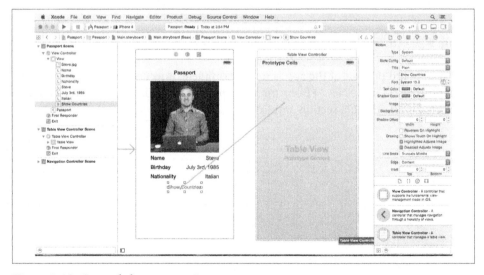

Figure 5-20. Control-drag connection

A pop-up menu will appear (Figure 5-21). Select Push from the menu and notice the new line connecting the Passport Scene and the Table View Controller Scene.

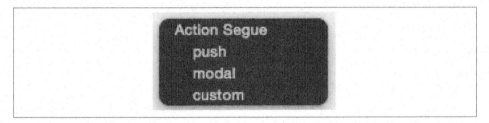

Figure 5-21. Connection pop-up

Also, notice the Table View Controller Scene now has a navigation bar. Double-click the navigation bar and type **"Countries Visited"**.

Select the white bar just under the words "Prototype Cells." In the Attributes Inspector, type **reuseIdentifier** into the Identifier input box (Figure 5-22).

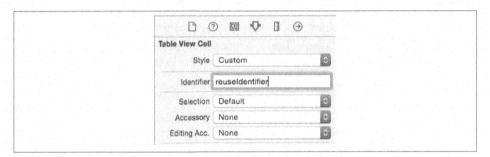

Figure 5-22. Attributes Inspector for Table View Cell

The storyboard portion of the app is nearly complete; now create the table view controller file. Select File→New→File from the top menu bar (Figure 5-23). Verify Source is selected under the iOS section and Cocoa Touch Class is selected; then click Next.

Figure 5-23. New file

It is now time to name the new class that will act as the table view's controller (Figure 5-24). But first, inside the "Subclass of:" input box, select UITableViewController. This will make the new class a subclass of `UITableViewController`. `UITable ViewController` does most of the heavy lifting for you. Now in the class input box, type **CountriesTableViewController**. Leave "Also create .xib" unselected and verify the language is set to Swift.

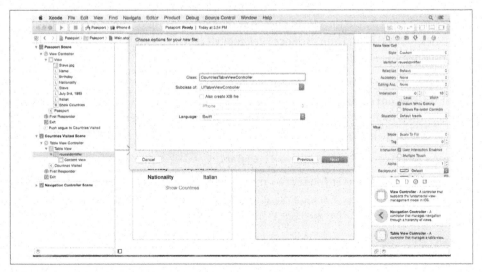

Figure 5-24. Name the new class

The next dialog will ask where you would like to save the new controller file. The current project directory should already be selected. Verify the Passport folder is at the top and click Create (Figure 5-25).

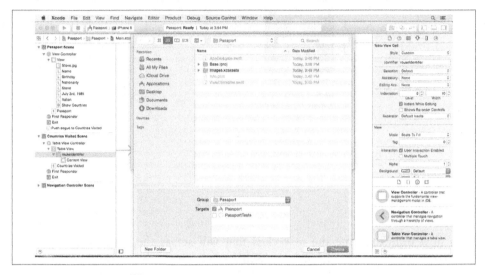

Figure 5-25. Save new file

The new *CountriesTableViewController.swift* file will automatically be opened inside of Xcode.

Then scroll down and highlight all of the green code at the bottom of the file and delete it. Be sure not to delete the closing brace at the very bottom of the file. Then highlight and delete viewDidLoad and didReceiveMemoryWarning as well. Then hide the Inspector and open the Project Navigator.

Place your cursor below the line that reads class CountriesTableViewController: UITableViewController. This is where properties are declared. The countries visited will be stored in an array. This array will be declared as a property, so any method will have access to it. To declare the array, type the following:

```
var countries = ["Italy","Norway","England"]
```

The numberOfSectionsInTableView method specifies the number of sections to be shown in the table view. Change the 0 to a 1. Remove the line that reads //#warning Potentially incomplete method implementation:

```
override func numberOfSectionsInTableView(tableView: UITableView) -> Int {
        //Return the number of sections.
        return 1
}
```

Below the `numberOfSectionsInTableView` method is the `numberOfRowsInSection` method. This method specifies the number of rows to be shown in the table view. Change the 0 to a 3. Remove the line that reads `//#warning Potentially incomplete method implementation`:

```
override func tableView(tableView: UITableView, numberOfRowsInSection section:
    Int) -> Int {
        //Return the number of sections.

        return 3
}
```

Place your cursor just below the two methods and type **tableView**. Autocomplete will appear and begin to assist you as you type. Highlight the line that reads:

```
tableView(tableView: UITableView, cellForRowAtIndexPath indexPath: NSIndexPath)
-> UITableViewCell
```

Then press Return and erase the code placeholder.

The `cellForRowAtIndexPath` method is called for each row inside the `tableView`. It creates the `UITableViewCell` and assigns text for each cell. Add the following line into the new method:

```
let cell = tableView.dequeueReusableCellWithIdentifier
("reuseIdentifier", forIndexPath: indexPath) as UITableViewCell
```

This line creates a constant called `cell` and sets it equal to a recycled cell from the `tableView`. The method checks if there are recycled cells available with the `reuseIdentifier` identifier. If there is a cell available, it sets `cell` to the recycled cell; otherwise, it creates a new cell. Next, add the following line of code:

```
var country = countries[indexPath.row]
```

This line of code sets a country name to the `country` variable. The `cellForRowAtIndexPath` method is called for each row in the table view. Each time it is called, the `indexPath` variable is updated to provide the section and row number. For example, the first time `cellForRowAtIndexPath` is called, it is for the first row in the first section, then the second row in the first section, and then the third row in the first section. This continues through each and every section. The `indexPath.row` variable is used to pull the first, second, or third country from the array.

Then add the following line of code:

```
cell.textLabel.text = country
```

This line of code takes the `country` variable and sets it to the `UITableViewCell`'s text. The country's name will now be displayed on the newly created cell.

Add the final line of code:

```
return cell
```

The application is almost complete; however, one more change must be made inside of the storyboard. Open *Main.storyboard* and open the Inspector.

Next, click the Table View Controller Scene then double-click the yellow circle at the top. A blue box will surround the yellow circle when it is selected. Then open the Identity Inspector. The Identity Inspector is the third icon from the left. It looks like a small newspaper. Inside the class input box, type **CountriesTableViewController** (Figure 5-26).

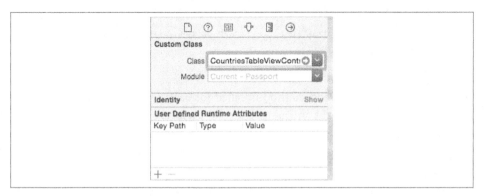

Figure 5-26. CountriesTableViewController custom class

This will attach the *CountriesTableViewController.swift* file to the Table View Controller Scene. The application is now complete; save your work and click the Play button in the upper left.

The app will launch and display the name, birthday, nationality, and photo as designed (Figure 5-27). Tap on the Show Countries button, and the navigation controller will push a new view controller onto the stack.

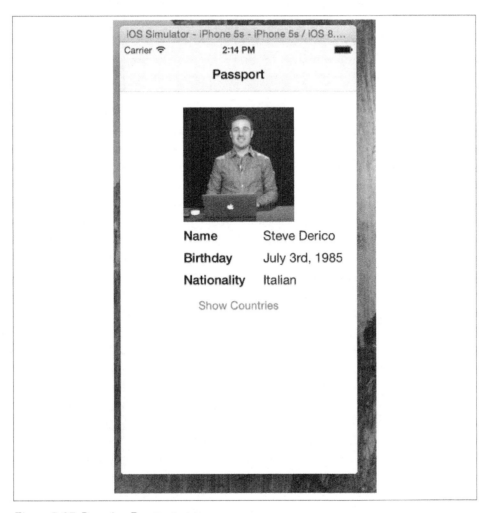

Figure 5-27. Running Passport app

Notice each cell shows a different country (Figure 5-28). The back button in the upper-left corner is automatically created. The back button will use the title from the previous view controller, or it will state "Back" if there is no title provided. Click the Back button.

Figure 5-28. Countries visited

Personal Challenge
What changes need to be made to have this app show five countries? What about 10 countries? What about 1,000 countries?

Don't worry if you received an error, warning, or your app did not run as expected. The
best way to learn is to make mistakes. Practice makes perfect. A sample version of the
project is available on AppSchool.com/book. Download it, compare, and try, try again.
Don't be scared to start the exercise over and walk through it until you get it right.

CHAPTER 6

Next Steps: Debugging, Documentation, and App Icons

In this chapter, you will learn how to debug your code. Debugging is a critical item in any developer's tool belt. The ability to debug properly can save you hundreds of hours. You will also learn how to read Apple's documentation. The documentation is like an encyclopedia provided by Apple; it has the answers to all your tough questions. Finally, you will learn how to add an app icon and a launch image to your apps. Let's keep building your knowledge base and get started.

Why Debugging?

A major part of developing software is making mistakes and solving issues. Issues, also known as *bugs*, are defined when an application is not running as expected. The process used to triage and troubleshoot issues is called *debugging*. Apple even provides a suite of tools inside of Xcode to assist with debugging.

Debugging is part of the development process; no matter how many apps you make, you will always have to debug. Just like spell check in Microsoft Word, just because you have written 500 essays doesn't mean you won't make spelling or grammar mistakes. Don't be discouraged when you are debugging; remember it is part of the process, and you are improving the quality of your app.

There are two major types of issues: compile time and runtime.

Compile-Time Issues

To understand compile-time issues, you must understand how Xcode works behind the scenes. Xcode takes the Swift code and translates it into zeros and ones in order for an iOS device to understand it. This translation from Swift to zeros and ones is called *compiling*, also known as *building*. It is important when your code is written that it builds properly; if it doesn't build properly, your app will not launch and will not be able to run. Whenever you click the Play button in the upper-left corner of the screen, the build process is started. If the build succeeds, then the app is run in the simulator. If it fails, Xcode will show a red error. For example, take a look at this code:

```
var total = 100 + 40
var half = totla / 2
```

The second line in the code has a compile-time error; there is no variable declared with the name `totla`. This would trigger an error, and the build would fail. See Figure 6-1.

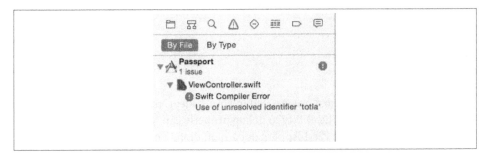

Figure 6-1. Issue Navigator

Xcode will also tell you the reason why the error was created. For example:

```
var total = 100 + 40
var half = totla / 2

//Use of Unresolved Identifier 'totla'
```

The reasons can sound a bit cryptic at first, but after a little while, it becomes more natural. In this case, Xcode is stating that an identifier, also known as a *variable*, is being used, but the variable is not found. This message translates to, *"You are using a variable that doesn't exist."* The variable `totla` doesn't exist because of a spelling error. Changing `totla` to `total` will resolve the issue:

```
var total = 100 + 40
var half = total / 2

//Build Successful - No Errors
```

Do not be discouraged by issues. There will be issues that take minutes, hours, or even days to solve. But remember, making mistakes and solving them is the best way to learn. There is no better feeling than solving an issue that once looked impossible. A positive attitude and a little persistence go a long way.

Errors

A compile-time error could be a problem with the syntax, accessing a property, or matching the proper type. These issues are caught by Xcode and are highlighted with a red dot, and an exclamation point will appear on the left side of the faulty line. Xcode's compile-time check is like Microsoft Word's grammar and spell checking. If there is an error, the error is highlighted and suggested solutions are provided.

Xcode has the ability to suggest solutions to problems, called a *Fix-It*. If there is a suggested fix, the red dot will appear, but instead of an exclamation point, there will be a white dot. Click the white dot, and a small pop-up menu will appear. This menu will state the issue and a possible fix. Click the *Fix-It* option, and the proposed fix will automatically be added to your code.

Warnings

In some cases, Xcode may suspect an issue could arise during runtime. In this case, Xcode will issue warnings. This could be because the type for a variable is not declared, or a variable could be unused. If a warning is found, a small yellow triangle will appear on the left side of the faulty line. Click the warning to reveal the possible issue. More often than not, warnings are indeed important and should be treated like errors.

When the application is built, the number of errors and warnings are shown at the top of Xcode. If there are any errors, Xcode will stop building and present a Build Failed notice (Figure 6-2). However, if there are warnings but no errors, Xcode will continue to build and provide a notice that the build was successful. All errors and warnings are collected and organized in one location, the Issue Navigator.

Figure 6-2. Build Failed notice

The Issue Navigator is available on the left window inside of Xcode. Reveal the Issue Navigator by clicking the fourth icon from the left in the Project Navigator's toolbar. The icon looks like a triangle with an exclamation point in it. Once the Issue Navigator is revealed, all the issues, errors, and warnings inside the project will be displayed in a list. Click the issue in question, and the Editor will automatically open the necessary file and highlight the problematic line of code. The Issue Navigator will also provide a description of the problem for each issue. This makes finding related issues much easier.

Runtime Issues

Runtime is when the application is running and the view is active. For example, a runtime issue could mean that the application is crashing whenever a particular button is tapped. Solving runtime errors can be more difficult than solving compile-time errors. It can be difficult to understand which line of code is executing if the application is currently running. This is where breakpoints are helpful. Breakpoints allow the developer to temporarily pause the application while it is running and watch the code execute line by line. The process used to go from line to line is called *stepping*. Stepping through your code is like watching an instant replay in slow motion. You can see the replay frame by frame and get a better sense of what is happening.

A *crash* is when the app cannot handle an issue that occurs when it is running. This results in the app shutting down and the user losing access.

Breakpoints

The left side of the editor is called the *gutter*. To create a breakpoint, click in the gutter next to the line of code you would like to debug. A dark blue rectangle with a pointer on it will appear (Figure 6-3). This signals the application will pause here during the code execution.

Figure 6-3. Breakpoint

If a breakpoint is set and is active on the line of code that is currently executing, the application will stop and show the Debugger.

A new pane will display from the bottom called the *debug area* (Figure 6-4). The debug area has two parts: the variables view and the console. The variables view, located on the left side of the debug area, displays the current variables in the method.

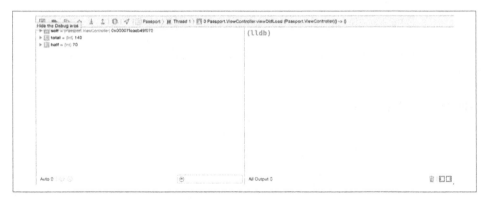

Figure 6-4. Debug area

Right-click a variable and select "Print description of variable" to print a detailed description of the variable to the console. The console on the right side of the debug area displays the developer log as the application is running (Figure 6-5). The console is a great way to monitor an application as it is running.

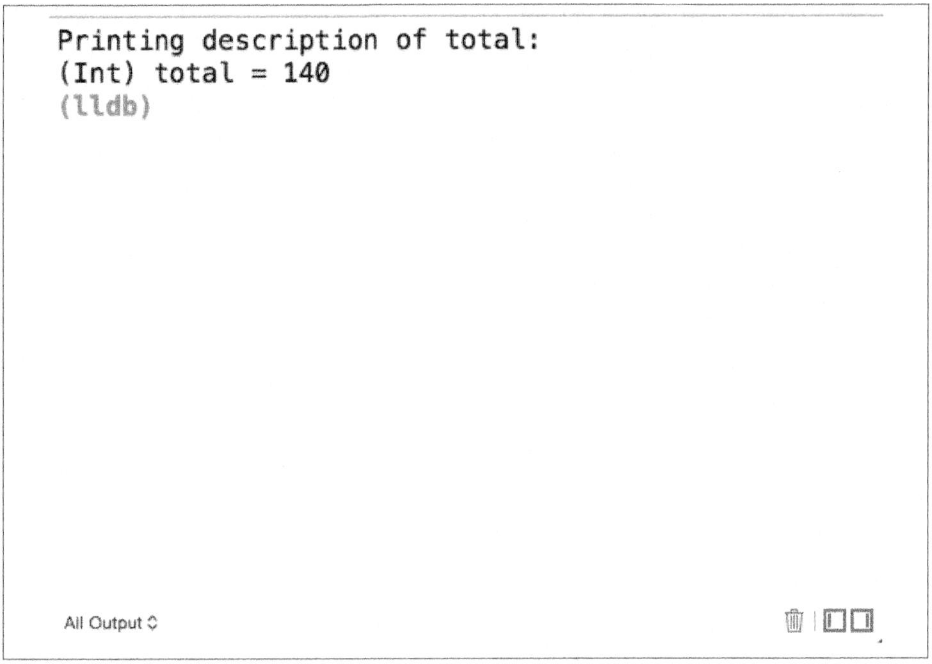

```
Printing description of total:
(Int) total = 140
(lldb)
```

All Output ↻   🗑 | ☐☐

Figure 6-5. Console

The `println()` method provides a simple way to print a message in the console. For example:

```
println("Button Tapped")
```

The `println()` method takes one parameter, a string, that is printed directly to the console when executed.

Using the Debugger

The variable view in Figure 6-6 is the debug toolbar. Table 6-1 shows each button on the debug toolbar from left to right.

Figure 6-6. Debug toolbar

Table 6-1. Debug toolbar buttons

Button	Description
Show/Hide	Debug area
Enable or Disable Breakpoints	Breakpoints
Continue	Resumes app back to normal state or until next breakpoint
Step Over	Executes next line of code, like a frame-by-frame forward button
Step Into	Moves the debugging into a method, if applicable
Step Out	Moves the debugging out of a method, if applicable
Debug View Hierarchy	Displays view for debugging interface elements and view layouts
Simulate Location	Selects a city to simulate GPS coordinates
Method Name	Shows the current method being called

The step over button will be used the most frequently. This button provides a slow-motion frame by frame of the code execution, like an instant replay. The console is also another helpful tool to determine when a particular event has happened or was logged.

Documentation

Documentation is the holy grail of any programming language. The documentation describes how each method, class, property, or variable works. The documentation is a developer's best friend and will help to provide required details like parameter types or return values for a particular method. Apple invests a large amount of time and resources into its documentation. If you have a question, the first place to check is the documentation.

You can open the documentation by clicking Window in the top menu bar and selecting "Documentation and API Reference" (Figure 6-7). The documentation window will appear. It's a good habit to always have the documentation window open when you are developing.

Figure 6-7. Documentation menu bar

The documentation window works a bit like a web browser (Figure 6-8). Search for a topic in the large input box and select a result from the list. The three-lined button to the left of the input box is the table of contents pane. This pane will display all the titles and sections the documentation has to offer for a particular subject. It also serves as a great tool to quickly navigate to a particular section. The small triangle inside the next button to the left shows the Library Navigator. The Library Navigator allows you to browse through the documentation instead of search. The forward and back buttons work as you would expect.

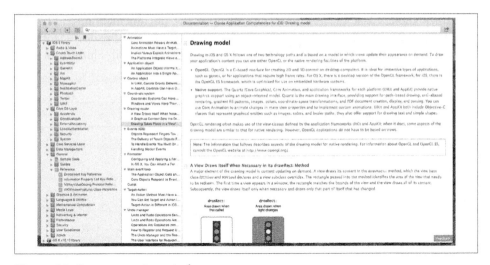

Figure 6-8. Documentation window

Finally, the main window will reflect the class, reference, or guide selected. In the case of a class, the documentation will provide a brief description of the class and then list all of the methods and properties available. Each method or property will have its description and example declaration. For methods, a description for each parameter and the return value is given. Finally, the documentation will state when the property or method was created (for example, "created in iOS 3.0").

Sample Code

The documentation provides more than just documents and guides. The documentation also provides sample code and example projects from Apple. These example projects are a great way to learn and see how Apple's technologies work together. For example, open the Library Navigator and open the iOS 8 library by clicking on the arrow. Open User Experience and then Sample Code and select HelloWorld. This is a sample project to show developers how to create a simple app that receives user input and display it on the user interface. Click Open Project to view the sample code.

How to Get the Most Out of Documentation

Every good developer puts time and energy into learning the documentation. This is the best way to become a more complete developer. Since the documentation is such an important piece of everyday development, there are a few tips and tricks you should know.

If you have a question about a particular class, keyword, or method, hover your mouse over it, hold the Option key, and click it. A Quick Help pop-up will be displayed (Figure 6-9). Here you will find the declaration, description, and a link to the Reference

Documentation. Click the reference link to open the documentation, or Option–double-click the item to avoid the Quick Help and go straight to the documentation. Also, you can open the documentation by pressing Command+Shift+0 on your keyboard.

Figure 6-9. Quick Help

One of the most valuable pieces of information inside the documentation is the iOS Human Interface Guidelines (*http://bit.ly/1xBts0t*). The iOS Human Interface Guidelines is a document that explains how to use the interface elements provided by Apple. This document is a must-read, and apps can be rejected from the App Store if they do not comply.

Every good developer is familiar with the documentation. You should make reading the documentation part of your development process. Understanding and learning the documentation is a skill that must be practiced. Browse the documentation to learn more about what frameworks and resources are available to you. Use the Library Navigator to dive into new topics and learn more.

App Icons

The app icon represents the app in the App Store, on the Home Screen, and even in Spotlight. The app icon is used in many sizes across many devices. The app icon sizes in Table 6-2 are required.

Table 6-2. Required universal app icons

Filename	Image size (px)	Description
iTunesArtwork.png	1024x1024	App Store Listing
Icon-60@3x.png	180x180	Retina HD Home Screen
Icon-60@2x.png	120x120	Retina Home Screen
Icon-76@2x.png	152x152	iPad Retina Home Screen
Icon-76.png	76x76	iPad Home Screen
Icon-40@3x.png	120x120	Retina HD Spotlight
Icon-40@2x.png	80x80	Retina Spotlight
Icon-40.png	40x40	Spotlight
Icon-29@3x.png	87x87	Retina HD Settings
Icon-29@2x.png	58x58	Retina Settings
Icon-29.png	29x29	Settings

More details on Retina and Retina HD will be provided in Chapter 7. It is highly recommended to name the files using the provided filenames. If they are not named properly, the icons can be easily confused during the import process. Once all the icons have been created, they must be added into Xcode.

To add the icons to Xcode, open the Project Navigator and click *images.xcassets*. This will open a bar on the left side of the Editor. Select AppIcon and a graph similar to a family tree will appear (Figure 6-10).

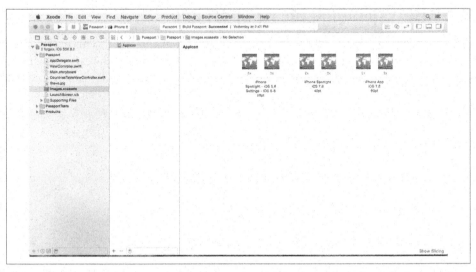

Figure 6-10. App icons

Drag each icon into its corresponding slot. Test the new icons by running the app in the iOS Simulator. After the app launches, from the top menu bar, select Hardware→Home, or Command+Shift+H, and the app icon will be displayed on the Home Screen.

Launch Image

A launch image is shown immediately when an app is launched. The launch image tells the user the app has launched and is currently loading. Without a launch image, the user will see a black screen and be left wondering if the app is actually working. Launch images are typically set to portrait orientation; however, a landscape launch image can also be provided. The best launch images are plain images that are similar to the first interface shown upon launch. For example, the Facebook app shows a light gray screen with a dark blue bar at the top.

Xcode automatically creates a launch image with your project. The *LaunchScreen.xib* file is used to define the look and feel for your app's launch image. The *LaunchScreen.xib* file also uses Auto Layout, explained more in the next chapter, to properly position elements on different device sizes.

In this chapter, you learned how to debug your code. You can now solve issues faster than before. You also learned how to read the documentation. Make reading the documentation part of your everyday development process. The more you read the documentation, the wider the net of apps you can build. Finally, you learned how to add your own app icon and a launch image to your apps. Keep up the great work and move on to the exercise.

Exercise: Expanding the Passport App

This exercise will expand on the Passport app created in Chapter 5. This exercise will also walk through using the Debugger and documentation. Finally, the exercise will add app icons and a launch image to the app (Figure 6-11).

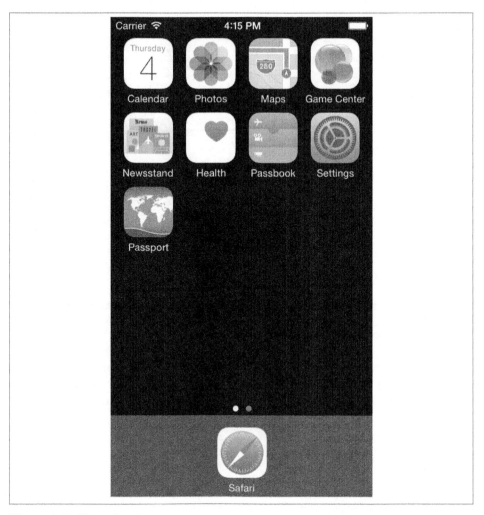

Figure 6-11. Home Screen

To get started, open Finder and then open the Passport project folder (Figure 6-12).
Inside the folder there are three items. There are two folders and a *Passport.xcodeproj*
file. Open the Passport folder.

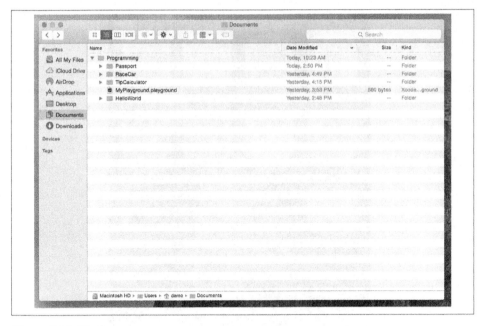

Figure 6-12. Finder

The files shown in Figure 6-13 make up the application. The file hierarchy shown here is not the same as the file hierarchy shown in the Project Navigator inside Xcode. The Project Navigator's organization and file hierarchy is purely superficial.

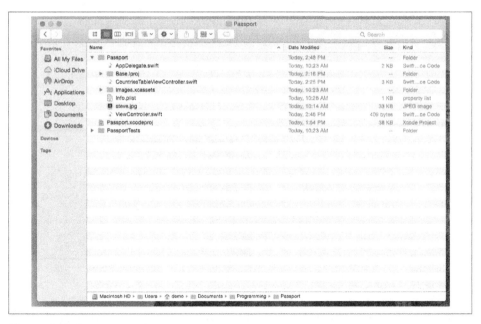

Figure 6-13. Passport project

Three *.swift* files are shown; these files are named for the classes they represent. The *Base.lproj* folder holds the *.storyboard* file, and *image.xcassets* holds the app icons. Finally, the *Info.plist* file is used to store details about the app, like version number and the bundle identifier. Go back and double-click the *.xcodeproj* file to get started.

It is time to add another country to the list of countries shown in your Passport app. Open the *CountriesTableViewController.swift* file and place your cursor after "England" in the countries array. Then type a space followed by "Spain"; be sure this is all inside the brackets of the array. Click the Play button in the upper-left corner of your screen.

Oops! It appears there is an error with the code. Click the red dot on the left side, and a Fix-It will appear (Figure 6-14). Click the Fix-It, and a comma will be properly inserted into the array. Click the Play button in the upper-left corner of your screen.

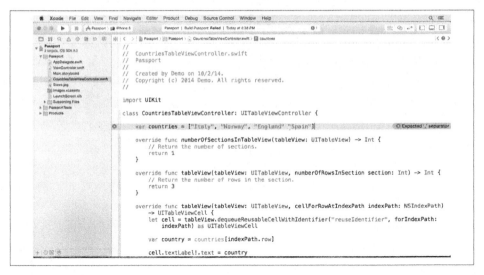

Figure 6-14. Error

When the app opens, tap the Show Countries button to view your new set of countries (Figure 6-15).

Figure 6-15. Countries visited

The country Spain is not properly displaying in the table view. Close the iOS Simulator and go back to the *CountriesTableViewController.swift* file.

Scroll down to the `cellForRowAtIndexPath` method. Place your cursor under the line that reads `cell.textLabel.text = country`. On the left side of the Editor is a light gray area just before the Project Navigator. This area is called the *gutter*; click inside the gutter just below the `cell.textLabel.text = country` line to create a breakpoint.

A blue arrow will appear on the left side of the Editor; this is the breakpoint (Figure 6-16). The breakpoint will pause the app and allow you to step through the creation of each row. This way you can get to the bottom of this issue. Click the Play button in the upper-left corner to get started.

Figure 6-16. Setting a breakpoint

Once the app has started, click the Show Countries button. You will notice the Simulator is hidden, and Xcode is brought back into view. The breakpoint line is highlighted in green, and the Debugger is shown at the bottom of the Xcode window (Figure 6-17).

Figure 6-17. Debug area

On the left side of the Debugger is a list of variables called the *variables view*. Notice the country variable is currently set to "Italy". Click the Continue button on the debug toolbar. The Continue button is the third icon from the left and looks like a Play button.

A loading indicator will appear quickly, and the green line will highlight the breakpoint line again. Look inside the variables view; the country variable is now set to "Norway". Click the Continue button on the debug toolbar.

A loading indicator will reappear quickly, and the green line will highlight the breakpoint line again. Look inside the variables view; the country variable is now set to "Eng land". Click the Continue button on the debug toolbar.

The simulator reappears, and the same three countries are shown in the table view. The debugging session shows that cellForRowAtIndexPath is only being called three times.

Reopen *CountriesTableViewController.swift* and remove the breakpoint from the gutter. Take a look at numberOfRowsInSection and notice the return value is currently set to three. This means only three cells will be created. Replace the return line with the following code:

```
return countries.count
```

This new return line will provide the exact number of elements inside the countries array. Now there will always be a cell for each element in the countries array. Click the Play button in the upper-left corner to verify.

Congratulations—you just fixed your first bug!

Documentation

It would be nice if the cells displayed something other than just the country name. Scroll down to the cellForRowAtIndexPath method. Hold the Option key and click UITable ViewCell. A small Quick Help box will appear (Figure 6-18). Click the *UITableViewCell Class Reference* link.

Figure 6-18. Quick Help

The UITableViewCell documentation window will appear. On the left side is a table of contents. Scroll down and click accessoryType. The documentation states:

> The accessory view appears in the right side of the cell in the table view's normal (default) state. The standard accessory views include the disclosure chevron; for a description of valid accessoryType constants, see UITableViewCellAccessoryType.

Click UITableViewCellAccessoryType, and a list of values will appear:

- None
- DisclosureIndicator
- DetailDisclosureButton
- Checkmark
- DetailButton

A checkmark on the right side of each country would be great. Close the documentation and place your cursor under the cell.textLabel.text = country line. Add the following code:

```
cell.accessoryType = .Checkmark
```

Click the Play button and notice the checkmark next to each country in the table view (Figure 6-19).

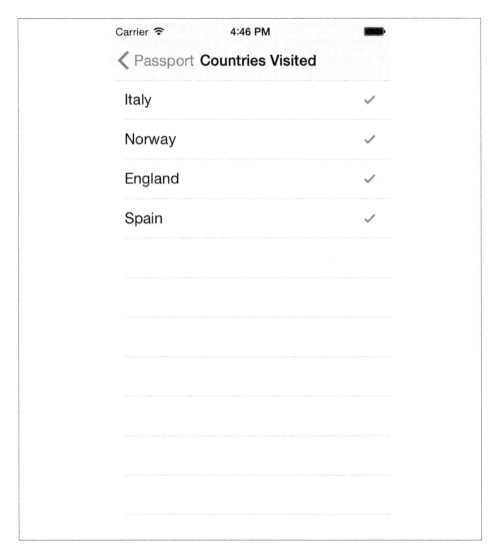

Figure 6-19. Checkmarks

Congratulations—you just learned your first lesson from the documentation.

App Icon

It is now time to add an app icon to the project. Download the app icons from *http://www.AppSchool.com/book*.

Next, open Xcode alongside Finder. Drag the upper-right corner of the Xcode screen to make room for Finder (Figure 6-20). Inside the Project Navigator, click *Images.xcassets* and then click AppIcon. Drag the AppIcon sidebar to reveal all the icon slots if necessary.

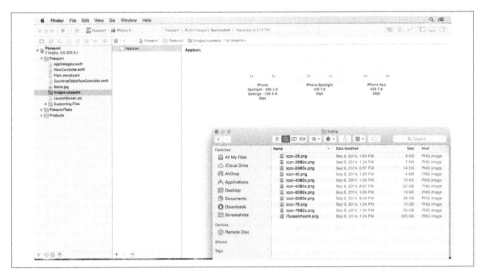

Figure 6-20. Finder and Xcode

Drag each file to the corresponding slot (Figure 6-21).

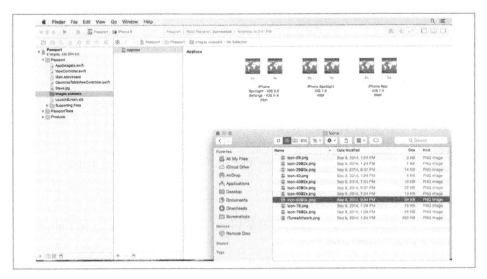

Figure 6-21. New app icons

The app icon installation is now complete.

Open the *LaunchScreen.xib* file and remove the Passport Label (Figure 6-22). Select the Label and press Delete. Launch the application in the iOS Simulator.

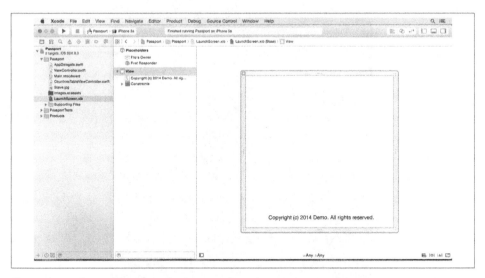

Figure 6-22. LaunchScreen.xib

Select Hardware→Home from the top menu bar to close the app and view the app icon (Figure 6-23).

Figure 6-23. New app icon

Don't worry if you received an error, a warning, or your app did not run as expected. The best way to learn is to make mistakes. Practice makes perfect. A sample version of the project is available on AppSchool.com/book. Download it, compare it, and try, try again. Don't be afraid to start the exercise over and walk through it until you get it right.

CHAPTER 7

Devices and Auto Layout

In this chapter, you will learn how to design an app with an interface for multiple devices. You will be introduced to all of Apple's devices and device sizes. This chapter will give you a foundation in app design so that you can start designing the user interface for your own apps.

Screen Sizes

iOS runs on many different device sizes and formats, including iPhone, iPod Touch, iPad, and iPad Mini. Table 7-1 contains all of these devices and their size in pixels.

Table 7-1. Device sizes

Device	Height (px)	Width (px)
iPhone	480	320
iPhone 4 (Retina)	960	640
iPhone 5 (Retina)	1136	640
iPhone 6 (Retina)	1334	750
iPhone 6 Plus (Retina HD)	1920	1080
iPad	1024	768
iPad w/ Retina	2048	1536
iPad Mini	1024	768
iPad Mini w/ Retina	2048	1536

Retina Displays

Pixels represent the drawable units on a display, just like the boxes on a sheet of graph paper. As devices have evolved, more and more pixels have been added. This creates a more dense area of pixels, providing more detail for each square inch of the device. This pixel-per-inch (PPI) is the standard for measuring the density of a display. When Steve Jobs announced the iPhone 4, he claimed the human eye could not notice the difference above a 300 PPI display. The iPhone 4 boasted a 326 PPI, and the term *Retina* has been used to describe any PPI over 300. The iPhone 6 Plus boasts a 401 PPI Retina HD display.

To help manage the Retina and Retina HD images for your application, Apple has provided some filenaming keywords:

Image.png
> Standard-sized image for non-Retina displays

Image@2x.png
> Double-sized image for Retina displays

Image@3x.png
> Triple-sized image for Retina HD displays

If you use the *@2x* and *@3x* keywords, Xcode will automatically use your Retina or Retina HD images when needed.

Swift requires iOS 7 or newer. iOS 7 requires an iPhone 4 or newer. Since all phones from the iPhone 4 and newer have a Retina display, it is guaranteed that all iPhone-sized devices will have a Retina display or better. However, some iPads also run iOS 7, but are not guaranteed to have a Retina display. The iPad Mini and iPad 2 both run iOS 7 and have the same non-Retina display. This 1024 x 768 px display is the only non-Retina display you will need to consider when designing your app.

Orientation

There are many devices for iOS, and there are four orientations for each device. A device can be positioned in one of four possible orientations at a time:

Portrait
> Device is positioned so that the sides are longer vertically than horizontally and the home button is at the bottom of the device. This is the default orientation.

Portrait Upside Down
> Device is positioned so that the sides are longer vertically than horizontally and the home button is at the top of the device.

Landscape Left
> Device is positioned so that the top and bottom are longer horizontally than vertically and the home button is on the left of the device.

Landscape Right
> Device is positioned so that the top and bottom are longer horizontally than vertically and the home button is on the right of the device.

Each application must specify its supported orientations. A *supported orientation* is an orientation in which the application will update or adjust depending on the position of the device. By default, Portrait, Landscape Left, and Landscape Right are all enabled as supported orientations.

Universal Apps

Apps must adjust depending on the device. Apple provides three different formats to help support these adjustments.

The first format is an iPhone app. An iPhone app will run as designed on an iPhone or iPod Touch. However, an iPhone app can also be run on an iPad. Because the iPad has more pixels than an iPhone, the iPad will display the iPhone app in scaled mode. Scaled mode shows the app in an iPhone-sized window on the iPad. Scaled mode also offers the ability to scale up the iPhone app to fill the entire iPad display. However, this requires the iPhone design to be stretched and creates a low-resolution, or pixelated, effect.

The second format of app is an iPad app. An iPad app will only run on an iPad or iPad Mini. An iPad app cannot be run on an iPhone or iPod Touch. The iPad app is designed specifically for iPad and will not scale or stretch.

Finally, the third format is universal. A universal app is designed to run on any device: iPhone, iPod Touch, iPad, or iPad Mini. A universal app contains a specific interface for both iPhone- and iPad-sized devices. To help developers ensure their design works well on all device sizes, Apple created Auto Layout.

Auto Layout

Auto Layout is a set of tools used to size and position elements on the screen. A traditional system uses fixed coordinates and sizes, but Auto Layout uses rules to size and position elements. These rules are called *constraints*.

Constraints are rules for size or positioning, for example *the left side of the Label should be offset 20 pts from the left edge of the containing view*. This constraint-based system allows the elements on the interface to resize for any size display.

To place a Label in the bottom-right corner of an iPhone 5, a traditional system would set the Y-offset to 550, the X-offset to 250, the width to 50, and the height to 10 (Figure 7-1).

Figure 7-1. Traditional Label in bottom-right corner of screen in Portrait

This system works well until another display size or orientation is brought into consideration. If the display is rotated to Landscape Left, a traditional system will not change the coordinates of the Label, leaving it off the screen (Figure 7-2).

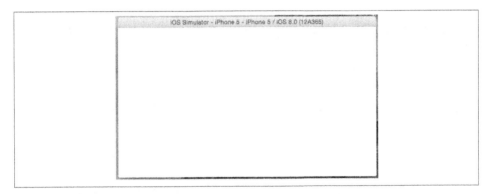

Figure 7-2. Traditional Label after Landscape Left rotate

If Auto Layout is used to position a Label in the bottom-right corner, it appears and acts the same in portrait or landscape (Figure 7-3).

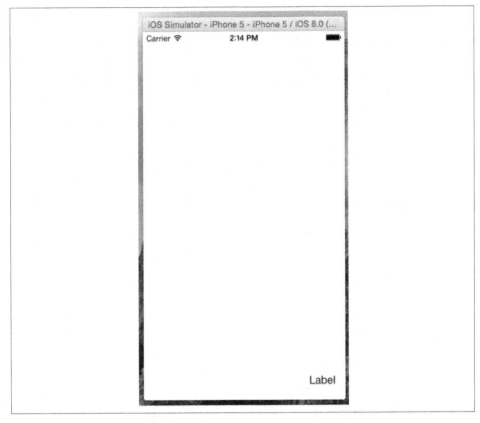

Figure 7-3. Label in bottom right with Portrait Auto Layout

Since Auto Layout uses constraints based on surrounding elements and edges, when the device is rotated into Landscape Left, the Label updates accordingly (Figure 7-4).

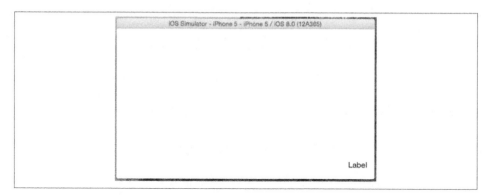

Figure 7-4. Label in bottom right with Landscape Auto Layout

Attributes

Constraints can be created based on a variety of different attributes. For example, you might want to position the right edge of a label 30 pts from the edge of the containing view (Figure 7-5). The containing view is the encapsulating view holding the elements together. Instead of positioning the right edge of an element, you can position many other attributes of an element.

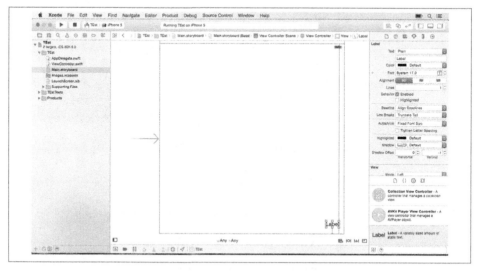

Figure 7-5. Storyboard with Label positioned via Auto Layout

The left, right, top, and bottom edges are common positioning attributes. For example, the English language reads from left to right. However, if the language you are presenting does not read left to right, like Arabic, the spacing should be flipped. In addition to the left and right attributes, Apple created the leading and trailing attributes. These attributes act as the left and right edges in a left-to-right language. They also act as the right and left edges in a right-to-left language.

Constraints can also be created based on the width, height, centerX, and centerY attributes. The width and height attributes are typically used to fix or set equal sizing across multiple elements. For example, you might have four buttons in a row across the bottom of the display. As the screen gets wider, the buttons should all grow to the same size.

The centerX and centerY attributes are used to position elements from the horizontal center or vertical center of an element. Finally, the baseline attribute is only available on elements with text. The baseline refers to the bottom boundary for a line of text.

Values

Each constraint must be set to a value. The value can be a specific number, a range of values, or the Standard Value. For example, on an iPhone, the Standard Value may be 20 pts, but for iPad, the Standard Value may be 25 pts. These values are set by Apple and vary based on device and orientation. Constraints can also be set to a specific number, for example, a constraint that offsets the leading edge of a Label by 30 pts. Auto Layout also supports ranges or inequalities as well. For example, consider a constraint setting the leading offset to be greater than or equal to 20 pts. This allows the leading offset to expand or lock as the container view changes. Finally, the Standard Value is the default spacing for that particular device.

Intrinsic Size

In some cases, it is necessary to allow an element to size itself. For example, a Label with a fixed width may clearly display the text "Tap here to enter." However, when the text is translated to German, "Tippen Sie hier, um geben," it is wider than its English translation. The fixed width of the Label will truncate the German text.

To avoid this issue, typically seen in Labels, Auto Layout has an Intrinsic Content Size option. This option provides organic sizing of the element based on the content. To enable this option, select a Label on the interface, select Editor from the top menu bar, and then click "Size to Fit Content."

Priority

In most cases, there will be many constraints for a given view. The elements on the screen will move relative to their size and constraints. In some cases, constraints can conflict with each other. A priority level is specified for each constraint to decide which constraint will take precedent.

Creating Constraints

Constraints are created inside of the storyboard file. When an element is dragged from the Object Library onto the interface, it is unconstrained. If the application is run without constraints, Xcode will pin the element to its absolute position. This means that if the containing view is resized, the elements will not move. To make the elements adjust to the change in size, constraints must be created. Each element should have a vertical and horizontal constraint. There are many ways to create constraints for your elements.

The Control-Drag Method

The most convenient way to create a constraint is to Control-drag between two elements. Select the element on the interface, hold Control, and drag the mouse from the element toward a neighboring element or edge. A small pop-up menu will be shown (Figure 7-6). Depending on the direction you drag, different options will be displayed.

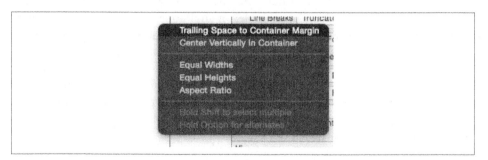

Figure 7-6. Pop-up constraint menu

If the drag is to the right, an option for the Trailing Space Constraint will be shown. If the drag is to the left, an option for the Leading Space Constraint will be shown. A left or right drag will also provide an option to align the element to the vertical center. A drag to the top will provide an option for the Top Space Constraint, and a drag to the bottom will provide an option for the Bottom Space Constraint. Finally, a top or bottom drag will also provide an option to align the element to the Horizontal Center.

Auto Layout Buttons

Constraints can also be created via the Auto Layout menu in the bottom-right corner of the Storyboard Editor (Figure 7-7). The Auto Layout menu is a group of four buttons used to help size and position elements using Auto Layout.

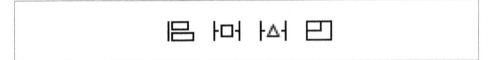

Figure 7-7. Auto Layout menu

The Align button

The first button from the left is the Align button. This button provides the ability to create alignment-based constraints, such as centering a view or aligning the edges of neighboring views.

To use the Align button, select an element and then click the first button in the bottom-left of your screen. The Align menu will appear and show a list of possible new constraints (Figure 7-8). Check the box next to the new constraint and enter the offset value in the text box on the right side. The text box also provides a drop-down menu with the Canvas and Standard Value options. The Canvas option will calculate the offset using the current position on the interface. The Standard Value will be determined by Apple's best practices and change depending on the device size. To complete the constraint, click Add Constraints.

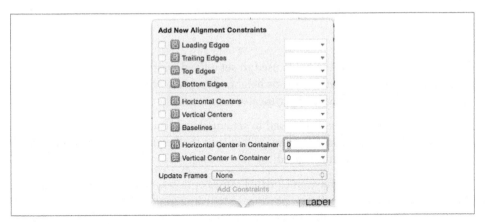

Figure 7-8. Align button menu

The Pin button

The next button is the Pin button. The Pin button creates constraints by defining spacing to the nearest neighbor or specifying a width or height. The Pin button has a few different sections from top to bottom.

The topmost section is used to create a new constraint based on a specific offset from the top, right, bottom, or left side of the selected element. The four input boxes receive the value, and a new constraint is created for each side of the element. The Pin menu can be tricky; the constraints will not be created unless the corresponding red line between the square and the input box is bolded (Figure 7-9). Once this red line is clicked, it will become bolded and the bottom of the menu will update with Add 1 Constraint.

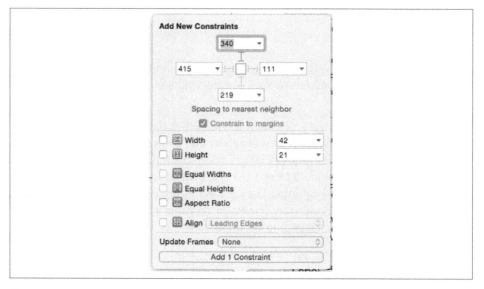

Figure 7-9. Pin menu

The second section from the top is used to set a fixed width or height to the element. Be careful when using fixed widths or heights, especially with Labels. The fixed width can result in the Label's text being truncated unexpectedly.

The third section from the top is used to set equal widths or heights across many elements, and the aspect ratio constraint will ensure the height and width aspect ratio is not changed if the element is resized.

The Align and Pin menus have an Update Frames option as well. This option will move the affected elements to their new positions according to the updated constraints. The update can be executed for all the elements in the container or just the elements affected by the new constraints.

Finally, the Align option inside the Pin menu is one of the most powerful and helpful ways to create constraints. With two elements selected, the Align option will provide a list of attributes to align between two elements. This is very helpful to ensure a set of left-aligned Labels are all stacked evenly on top of each other.

The Resolve Auto Layout Issues button

The third button is the Resolve Auto Layout Issues button. This button helps fix Auto Layout issues by providing suggestions and resetting constraints. It can analyze the view and create constraints based on the layout of the interface elements.

The Issues menu is divided into two menus, top and bottom (Figure 7-10). The top half only affects the selected element on the screen, while the bottom half affects all elements. The most helpful feature of the Issues menu is the "Reset to Suggested Constraints" option. This option will remove all the current constraints and create new constraints based on where the elements are positioned on the interface. This option serves as a great starting point, since the constraints can be edited after they are created.

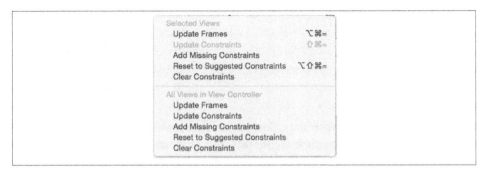

Figure 7-10. Issues menu

The Resizing Behavior button

The last button is the Resizing Behavior button. This button provides a menu to control how constraints are applied when resizing takes place (Figure 7-11). Depending on how many elements are selected, options in each menu may be disabled. For example, the equal widths option sets a group of elements to the same width. However, this option will not be enabled if only one element is selected.

Figure 7-11. Resizing Behavior menu

The Guidelines Method

When an element is positioned on the interface, guidelines are shown at the horizontal center, vertical center, and toward the edges of the interface (Figure 7-12). Using these guidelines can help Xcode to suggest and automatically create constraints for you.

Figure 7-12. Guidelines

To automatically create constraints, position an element on the interface while using one of the guidelines. Then click the Resolve Auto Layout Issues button; it features a triangle with wings. Once the Resolve Auto Layout Issues button is clicked, a small menu will appear. Scroll to the top and select "Reset to Suggested Constraints" (Figure 7-13). This option will tell Xcode to remove any existing constraints and create constraints based on the element's current positioning. Open the Document Outline to view all the constraints for the interface.

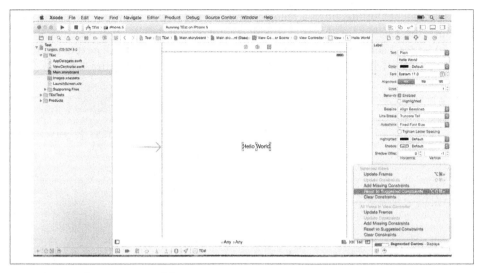

Figure 7-13. Element on guideline

Testing Layout Constraints

When positioning an element with Auto Layout, the constraints will change colors to provide feedback. If the constraints shown are orange, that means there are not enough constraints provided to properly position the element, or there is an error (Figure 7-14).

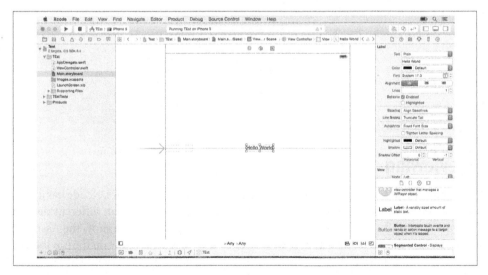

Figure 7-14. Orange constraints

The Document Outline shows a yellow triangle or red circle icon when there is an Auto Layout issue. Clicking on the Auto Layout error icon will show a list of the current Auto Layout issues. Each issue will be listed, and a reason will be provided; next to each issue will be a yellow triangle, a warning, or a red circle, for an error (Figure 7-15).

Figure 7-15. Constraint errors and warnings

Click on the icon next to the issue, and a Fix-It pop-up box will be shown (Figure 7-16). This pop-up box will present a suggested solution for the issue. Click the Fix button to automatically add the fix. Be sure to investigate the constraints added to your view via the Fix-It system, since sometimes they do not work for each device.

Figure 7-16. Constraint Fix-It

Previewing

It's important to test your interface in multiple device sizes and shapes. Xcode has a built in Previewer, which will show exactly how the interface will look on different devices (Figure 7-17). To show the Previewer, first hide the Inspector. Then show the Assistant Editor. Once the Assistant Editor is shown, click the word Automatic on the top toolbar of the Assistant Editor. A drop-down menu will appear; select Preview. The right side of your screen will now show a preview of the interface on a device. To add more devices, click the small plus icon in the bottom left of the Assistant Editor window.

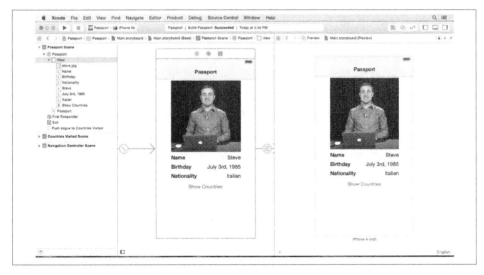

Figure 7-17. Previewer

Exercise: Building More on the Passport App

This exercise builds on top of the Passport app from Chapters 5 and 6. In this exercise, Passport will be updated to work with Auto Layout. The user interface will adjust to an iPhone or iPad in Landscape or Portrait orientation (Figure 7-18).

Figure 7-18. Finished exercise screenshot

Open the Passport project file inside Xcode. Click Passport in the Project Navigator, and the project details will appear. Scroll down and set Devices to Universal. Then check the Upside Down, Landscape Left, and Landscape Right boxes. Then open *Images.xcassets* and highlight AppIcon. Press Delete. Right-click in the white sidebar and select New App Icon. A new iPad and iPhone App Icon grid will appear. Open the Passport Icon folder and drag in the corresponding icons.

On the toolbar, click the iOS Simulator drop-down menu next to Passport.

The drop-down menu lists all the devices available in the iOS Simulator (Figure 7-19). Select iPad Air and click Play. The iOS Simulator will now launch in the form of an iPad Air.

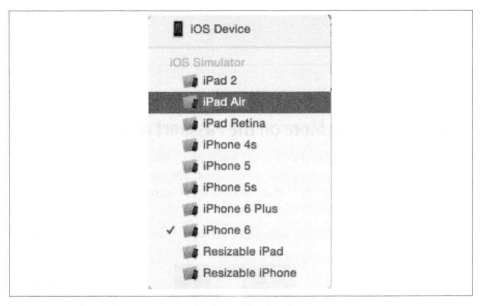

Figure 7-19. Drop-down devices

The iPad Air simulator is very large, especially on a small screen. To adjust this, go to the top menu bar and select Window→Scale→50% (Figure 7-20). The iPad Air simulator will now operate at half the standard size.

Figure 7-20. iPad Air drop-down menu

The Passport app does not look very pleasing on the iPad. The image has been moved, and the labels are offset (Figure 7-21). This is because the current positioning system works with fixed width and height coordinates.

Figure 7-21. iPad Air simulator

You will need to change the positioning system to Auto Layout. Open the *Main.storyboard* file and then select the File Inspector (Figure 7-22). Check the box Use Auto Layout and then Use Size Classes. Then click Enable Size Classes (Figure 7-23).

Figure 7-22. File Inspector

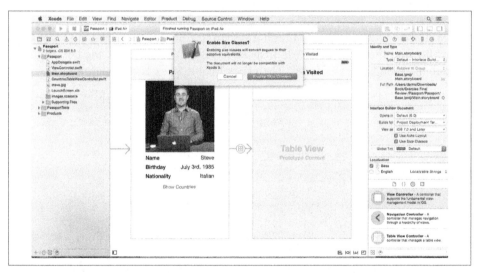

Figure 7-23. Enable Size Classes button

Size classes can be used to change layouts for different device sizes. The positioning system is now set to Auto Layout. To take advantage of Auto Layout, constraints must be added to each interface. Open the Passport Scene.

Position the Image View along the horizontal-center guideline. Then drag the Image View up to the top buffer guideline. Click the Align button and select Horizontal Center in Container; then Add 1 Constraint. Next, select the Pin button and from the top drop-down menu, select Use Standard Value. Then check the Width and Height options and click Add 3 Constraints (Figure 7-24).

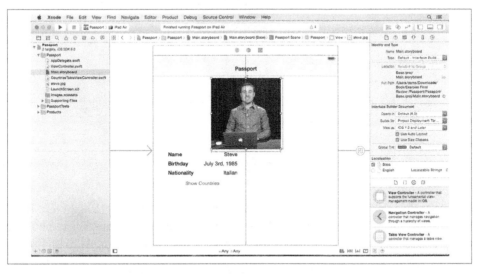

Figure 7-24. Repositioned Image View

Drag the three right-side Labels under the bottom-right corner of the Image View. Next, draw a box and select the right-side Labels along with the Image View. Click the Align button and check the Trailing Edges option. Then click Add Constraints. With just the right-side Labels selected, click the Pin button and select Use Standard Value from the top drop-down menu. Then from the Update Frames drop-down, select Items of New Constraints and click Add Constraints (Figure 7-25).

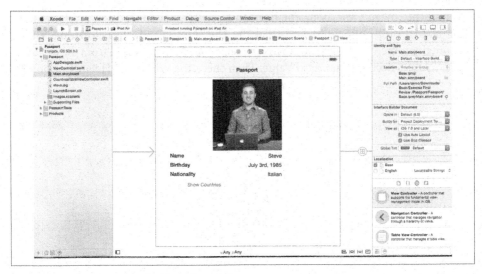

Figure 7-25. Repositioned right-side Labels

Drag the three left-side labels under the bottom-left corner of the Image View. Next, draw a box and select the left-side Labels along with the Image View. Click the Align button and check the Leading Edges option. Then click Add Constraints. With just the left-side Labels selected, click the Pin button and select Use Standard Value from the top drop-down menu. Then from the Update Frames drop-down, select Items of New Constraints and click Add Constraints (Figure 7-26).

Figure 7-26. Repositioned left-side Labels

Position the button along the horizontal center guideline. Then drag it up until it is placed just below the bottom Label's base guideline. Click the Align button and select Horizontal Center in Container and then Add 1 Constraint. Finally, click the Pin button and select Use Current Canvas Value from the top drop-down menu; then Add Constraint (Figure 7-27).

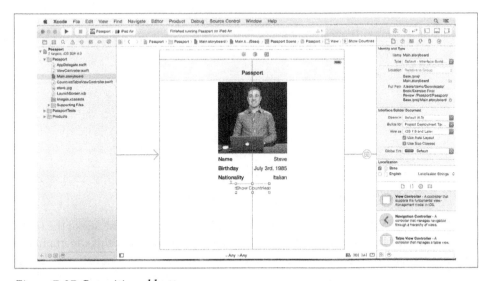

Figure 7-27. Repositioned button

These constraints will be used and inherited on all size classes and layouts. Now tweak and modify these constraints for a specific size class. Click "Any, Any" at the bottom of the screen. A small grid will appear; this controls which size class is currently being edited. Click the bottom right of the grid (Figure 7-28). This size class is used for iPads in Portrait or Landscape orientation.

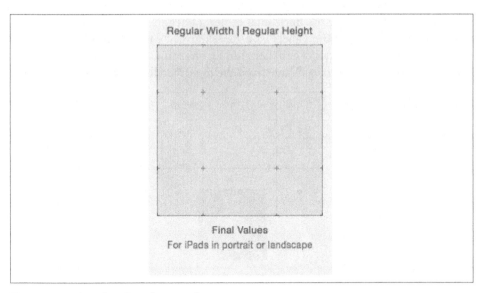

Figure 7-28. Regular, Regular size class

Select the Image View, and a blue vertical line will appear on the right side of the Image View. This is the height constraint for the Image View. Double-click this constraint and change its value from 225 to **400**. Next, double-click the horizontal line below the Image View; this is the width constraint. Change the width constraint's value from 225 to **400**. The Image View will resize, and the Labels and Buttons will reposition themselves (Figure 7-29).

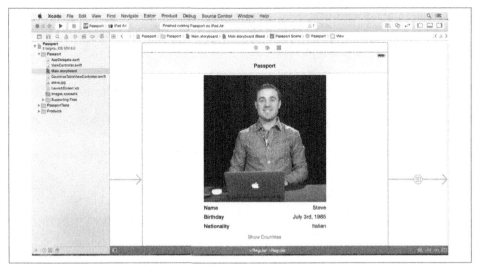

Figure 7-29. Resized Image View

To review these new constraints, use the Previewer. Before you open the Previewer, it is best to clear up some space; hide the Project Navigator and Inspector. Then open the Assistant Editor; its icon has two connected circles inside it. From the Assistant Editor toolbar, click Automatic. A drop-down menu will appear; select Preview→ Main.storyboard (Preview) (Figure 7-30).

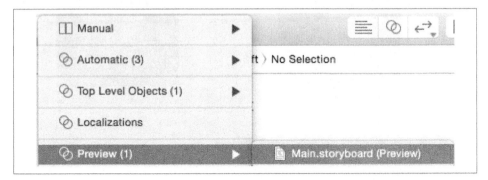

Figure 7-30. Preview menu

The right side of the Xcode screen will now show a live preview of the interface on a 4-inch iPhone. Click the plus button in the bottom-left corner and then iPad. An iPad preview will be added to the right side of the Previewer (Figure 7-31). The interface looks much better on the iPad. Rotate the preview by clicking the small arrow at the bottom of the iPad preview. Notice the interface rotates, and the elements are still positioned properly. Rotate the iPhone 4-inch preview. The elements on the screen are being cut off and are not properly displayed.

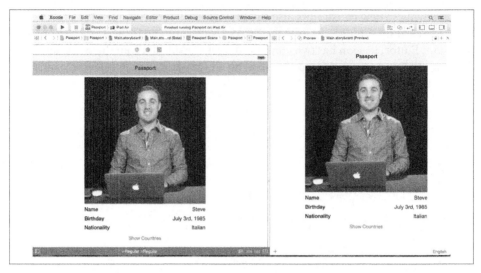

Figure 7-31. Previewer

Select the "Regular, Regular" link at the bottom of the screen and click the middle box in the top row of the grid. This will change the size class to "Any, Compact" (Figure 7-32). This size class is specifically for iPhones in Landscape. The interface will rotate, and some elements may be missing. To fix this, from the top menu bar, select Edit→Select All. All of the elements on the interface will be highlighted. Drag the Image View toward the top of the interface to reveal the missing elements.

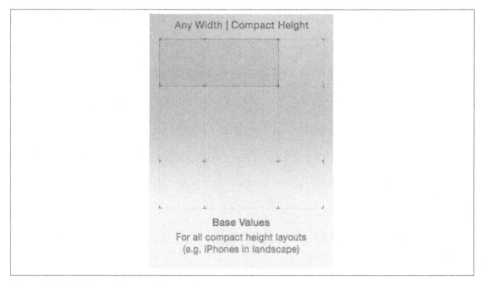

Figure 7-32. "Any, Compact" size class

This size class will require a completely new layout (Figure 7-33). Next, click the Resolve Auto Layout Issues button and then select Clear Constraints from the bottom of the menu; this will clear the current constraints only for this size class. Next, drag the Image View to the left-side guideline and then drag it up the top buffer guideline. With the Image View selected, click the Pin button and select Use Standard Value from the top drop-down menu and then select Use Current Canvas Value from the left drop-down menu. Then check the width and height checkboxes and select Add Constraints. Drag the Labels and Buttons and place them against the top buffer guideline; then drag them to the left until they touch the Image View's right buffer guideline. Finally, click the Pin button and select Use Standard Value from the top drop-down menu, and then select Use Current Canvas Value from the left drop-down menu. Then click Add Constraints.

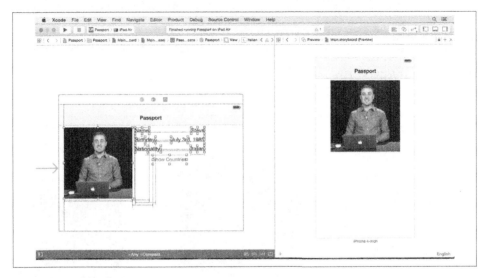

Figure 7-33. New layout

The app is now ready for testing; select iPhone 5s from the iOS Simulator drop-down menu and click the Play button. Rotate the simulator by selecting Hardware→Rotate Right from the top menu bar (Figure 7-34). Test the app with an iPad Air as well (Figure 7-35).

Figure 7-34. iPhone 5s Landscape screenshot

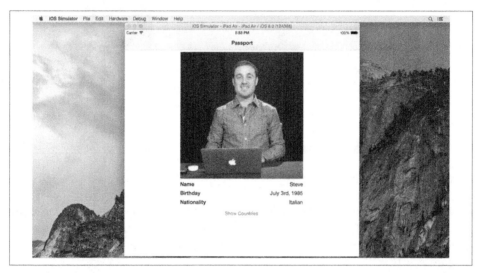

Figure 7-35. iPad Air screenshot

Don't worry if you received an error, a warning, or your app did not run as expected. The best way to learn is to make mistakes. Practice makes perfect. A sample version of the project is available on AppSchool.com/book. Download it, compare it, and try, try again. Don't be afraid to start the exercise over and walk through it until you get it right.

CHAPTER 8

Maps and Location

In this chapter, you will learn how to harness the power of the iPhone's Global Positioning System (GPS) inside your app. You will learn how to access the user's location and plot it on a map. This chapter will also cover Map Kit, Apple's framework for mapping and directions. With the information in this chapter, you will be able to tackle a location-based app in no time.

Providing information based on the user's location is one of the most exciting features available while developing with an iOS device. Displaying the user's location on a map is a two-step process. The first step is to gather the user's location using Core Location. *Core Location* is a set of classes designed to work with the device's GPS, cellular antenna, and WiFi antenna to provide the user's location. Core Location is one of many optional frameworks provided by Apple. *Frameworks* are a set of classes and tools designed for a specific task. Let's take Core Location as an example. It is a framework designed to work with location. Core Data is a framework designed to work with databases. These frameworks are optional, so they must be imported into the project to work properly.

The second step is to plot the user's location on a map. Apple provides a framework called *Map Kit* to help draw and manage maps. Xcode 6 makes importing frameworks easy. To import Map Kit, click a project name in the Project Navigator. Then select the Capabilities tab and scroll down to Maps. Toggle the Maps switch to On and notice that *MapKit.framework* has been added to the Project Navigator. The framework is now available in the project, but the import process is not complete. The framework must be imported into the controller file as well. To import a framework in Swift, use the import keyword followed by the proper name of the framework:

```
import MapKit
```

This process will import the Map Kit classes and protocols into the controller. Now Autocomplete will also show Map Kit classes and protocols. Map Kit classes and protocols start with *MK*.

Core Location

As you just learned, Core Location is a set of classes and tools designed to find the user's location. There are three methods of location detection via Core Location. The first method is Significant-Change Location. This method saves battery usage by only providing updates when the user's location has changed significantly. The second method is Location Services, offering a highly customizable way to locate the user and receive updates. Finally, the Regional Monitoring method uses nearby boundaries defined by geographic regions or Bluetooth beacons. This book will work with the second option, Location Services, since it is most commonly used.

More information is available in Apple's Location and Maps Programming Guide (*http://bit.ly/1zmUVCf*).

Accessing a user's location requires the Core Location framework. The Core Location framework is not automatically imported when the Maps capabilities switch is toggled to on. The framework must be manually imported. To import the Core Location framework:

1. Click the blue project icon in the Project Navigator.
2. Scroll down to the bottom of the project details.
3. Under Link Binary with Libraries, click Add.
4. Select Core Location and click Add.

The framework will be added to the Project Navigator. To access the framework, be sure to add the following `import` statement in the controller:

```
import CoreLocation
```

 Collecting the user's location is a power-intensive task. This means it requires more battery life and antenna power than other tasks. It is important that your app only uses Location Services as needed. As soon as the information needed is gathered Location Services should be turned off. In the case that more information is needed in the future, periodic updates are available.

Finally, before requesting the user's location, it is important to check if Location Services are available; Location Services may be unavailable if:

- The user has disabled Location Services in the Settings app.
- The user has denied Location Services access for your app.
- The device is in airplane mode or unable to connect externally.

Core Location provides a simple method called `locationServicesEnabled` to determine if Location Services are available. The `locationServicesEnabled` method returns a Boolean variable with the availability of Location Services.

Requesting User Location

Requesting the user's location is done via a class named `CLLocationManager`. The prefix, *CL*, stands for Core Location. The location manager is used to collect parameters and trigger Location Services. Creating a `CLLocationManager` object is similar to creating any other object. For example:

```
var locationManager: CLLocationManager = CLLocationManager()
```

`CLLocationManager` has a few properties that must be set for it to operate.

The `desiredAccuracy` property is an enumeration value. An *enumeration* value, or *enum*, is a keyword that represents a number. Enums are similar to multiple choice tests: you must pick one value from a list. The `desiredAccuracy` property accepts the following values:

`kCLLocationAccuracyBest`
Most accurate and most power-intensive option

`kCLLocationAccuracyNearestTenMeters`
Accurate within 10 meters

`kCLLocationAccuracyHundredMeters`
Accurate within 100 meters

`kCLLocationAccuracyKilometer`
Accurate within 1 kilometer

`kCLLocationAccuracyThreeKilometers`
Accurate within 3 kilometers

With more accuracy comes more power usage; choose the accuracy level that meets the minimum required level of information. If the app tracks the user on a map, like Google Maps, `kCLLocationAccuracyNearestTenMeters` or `kCLLocationAccuracyHundredMeters` will work well. However, if the app states the name of the city, like Twitter, `kCLLocationAccuracyKilometer`, or `kCLLocationAccuracyThreeKilometers` would be a great fit. For most situations, `kCLLocationAccuracyBest` is not required.

Setting the `desiredAccurracy` is similar to setting a property on any other object:

```
locationManager.desiredAccuracy = kCLLocationAccuracyHundredMeters
```

`CLLocationManager` also requires a `delegate` property. The `CLLocationManager` delegate follows the `CLLocationManagerDelegate` protocol. The delegate will receive alerts whenever there is a location update, or there is an error. To receive these alerts, the delegate must communicate via the CLLocationManagerDelegate protocol. The controller must declare it is following, or conforming, to the CLLocationManager Delegate. To declare the conformation to the protocol, add CLLocationManager Delegate to the top of the class:

```
class ViewController: UIViewController, CLLocationManagerDelegate
```

To receive location alerts, you must implement the locationManager(_:, didUpdate Locations:) method. This method will be called each time the location information is changed:

```
func locationManger(manager: CLLocationManager!,
didUpdateLocations locations: [AnyObject]!){
        println("Location found")
}
```

To receive updates whenever there is an error with Core Location, implement the loca tionManager(_: didFailWithError:) method:

```
func locationManager(manager: CLLocationManager!, didFailWithError error:
NSError!){
        println("Error!")
}
```

Once the new methods are implemented and the protocol conformation is complete, the delegate property must be set:

```
locationManager.delegate = self
```

Before Location Services are activated, the user must approve location sharing with the app. There are two types of Location Services approvals. The first is requestWhenInU seAuthorization; this authorization asks only for location information while the application is running in the foreground. The second authorization is requestAlwaysAu thorization. This authorization will provide the app with the ability to track the user's location if the app is in the foreground or the background. Calling these authorizations is a simple as calling a method:

```
locationManager.requestWhenInUseAuthorization()
```

or:

```
locationManager.requestAlwaysAuthorization()
```

Finally, after the authorization is requested, Location Services can be enabled by calling startUpdatingLocation():

```
locationManager.startUpdatingLocation()
```

The locationManager will then begin tracking and returning the user's location based on the information provided.

The `locationManager(_:, didUpdateLocations:)` method will provide an array of `CLLocations` in the order they occurred. There will always be at least one object in the array. Each object in the array is a `CLLocation`. `CLLocation` is a simple class that organizes a `CLLocationManager`'s location data for a specific location. `CLLocation` keeps track of geographical coordinates, altitude, speed, heading, and even the level of accuracy used for detection. `CLLocation` has some very helpful properties:

`coordinate`
> `CLLocationCoordinate2D`, latitude and longitude coordinates

`altitude`
> Altitude measured in meters

`timestamp`
> The time and date when the data was captured

`description`
> Returns the `CLLocation` in `String` format, great for `println()`

Remember, once you have the information needed, it is very important to stop Location Services. To stop the services, call `stopUpdatingLocation()` on the `CLLocation Manager`:

```
manager.stopUpdatingLocation()
```

For example, it is very common to stop Location Services after the location has been detected inside the `locationManager(manager:, didUpdateLocations:)` method. The manager variable points to the `CLLocationManager` created earlier and is a perfect variable to use for this situation.

Gotchas
The iOS 8 Simulator has shown some inconsistent behavior with Core Location. If Location Services are not being called, add the following three keys to the *Info.plist* file:

- `NSLocationWhenInUsageDescription`
- `NSLocationAlwaysUsageDescription`
- `NSLocationUsageDescription`

Set Always or When in Use as the value for each. These keys will help to enable and trigger Location Services.

Map Kit

Map Kit is a framework designed to provide maps and directions. These maps can display street-level information, 3D buildings, satellite imagery, or a combination of both. The maps also automatically respond to pinch, zoom, pan, and tilt. Points can be plotted on the map using annotations.

MKMapView

To display a map, Map Kit provides a simple view class called MKMapView. The MKMap View class displays a map, manages input from the user, and even shows custom annotations.

MKMapView also has a delegate property. Much like the delegate property on CLLocation Manager, MKMapView's delegate will receive updates as they happen. The MKMapView delegate must conform to the MKMapViewDelegate protocol. To set the delegate, Control-drag from the Map View in the Storyboard Editor over to the words "View Controller" in the Document Outline. A small pop-up menu will be shown. Click delegate, and the delegate will be set to the view controller associated with that interface.

MKMapView has many convenient properties and methods. For example, MKMapView comes with the ability to display a user's location on the map without adding any additional code. To enable the user's location on the map, set the showsUserLocation property to true:

```
myMapView.showsUserLocation = true
```

The user's location will now be displayed via a blue dot on the map.

It is common to set the user's location to the center of the map. To move and recenter the map to a new point, set the centerCoordinate property. The centerCoordinate property requires a CLLocationCoordinate2D. A CLLocationCoordinate2D is just the latitude and longitude coordinates wrapped into a single variable. You can create a CLLocationCoordinate2D using the CLLocationCoordinate2DMake method:

```
var coordinates: CLLocationCoordinate2D = CLLocationCoordinate2DMake(100,100)
```

Finally, it is common to zoom in on a location on a map. The zoom level is automatically adjusted when the region property is set. The region property requires a MKCoordinate Region object. However, in most cases, editing the current region object is easier than creating a new one:

```
var updatedRegion: MKCoordinateRegion = myMapView.region

updatedRegion.span.longitudeDelta = updatedRegion.span.longitudeDelta * 2.0
updatedRegion.span.latitudeDelta = updatedRegion.span.latitudeDelta * 2.0

myMapView.region = updatedRegion
```

The `longitudeDelta` and `latitudeDelta` values are part of the `span`. The `span` is how much area or width and height around the `centerCoordinate` to shown.

Directions

Map Kit also provides the ability to add turn-by-turn directions inside any app. The `MKDirections` API provides directions calculated by Apple's servers. These directions can provide walking or driving directions, travel time, and alternate routes. Each point on the map is represented by a `MKMapItem`. A `MKMapItem` contains all the information about a specific location on a map. This information includes map location, coordinates, and data like the name of the location. These `MKMapItems` can also be passed to the Maps app for more advanced features.

The easiest way to create a `MKMapItem` is to use the `mapItemForCurrentLocation` method. This method will take the user's location and create a `MKMapItem` from it:

```
var mapItem: MKMapItem = MKMapItem.mapItemForCurrentLocation()
```

The `MKMapItem` class has a few convenient properties. The `name` property is a string that provides a descriptive name. The `phoneNumber` property is a string that holds the phone number for the location. The `URL` property holds the website URL for a particular location.

Once the `MKMapItems` are created, it is very simple to share them with the Maps app and to provide turn-by-turn directions. The `openMapsWithItems:launchOptions:` method accepts an array containing one or more `MKMapItems`. These items will be mapped according to the `launchOptions`. The `MKLaunchOptionsDirectionsModeKey` tells the Maps app to provide directions between the two points.

Plotting Points

Apple provides a method to plot points on a map called *annotations*. Annotations are designed to define a single place or point. Annotations are often used to highlight points of interest and provide more detail. An annotation can also have an optional callout bubble. This bubble can present information like the location's name and address. Bubbles can also be actionable and serve as a button to receive user action.

Annotations are made up of two parts, the annotation object and the annotation view. The *annotation object* is a lightweight object that manages the data for the annotation. This annotation object is created from the `MKPointAnnotation` class. The *annotation view* is an object created from the `MKPinAnnotationView` class. The annotation view is used to draw the pin on the map.

There are three steps to adding an annotation to an MKMapView. The first step is to create a MKPointAnnotation for the point of interest:

```
var point = MKPointAnnotation()
point.coordinate = CLLocationCoordinate2DMake(37.7756, -122.4193)
point.title = "San Francisco"
```

Next, conform to the MKMapView protocol and respond to the mapView(_: viewForAnnotation:) method. This method manages the recycling of annotation views, much like in a table view:

```
func mapView(mapView: MKMapView!, viewForAnnotation annotation: MKAnnotation!)
  -> MKAnnotationView!{

      var pin = MKPinAnnotationView(annotation: annotation, reuseIdentifier:
    "pinIdentifier")
      return pin
}
```

Finally, call the addAnnotation method. This will add the annotation to the map:

```
mapView.addAnnotation(point)
```

You are now ready to tackle your first location-based app.

Exercise: Adding Maps to the Passport App

In this exercise, you will expand on the Passport app from previous chapters. You will add a new Map View, displaying a pin in each country visited (Figure 8-1). The Map View will be shown when the user taps the new Map button in the upper right of the Countries Visited screen.

Figure 8-1. Finished exercise screenshot

To get started, open the *Passport.xcodeproj* file. Click the project name in the Project Navigator. Then click Capabilities. Scroll down to Maps and turn it On (Figure 8-2).

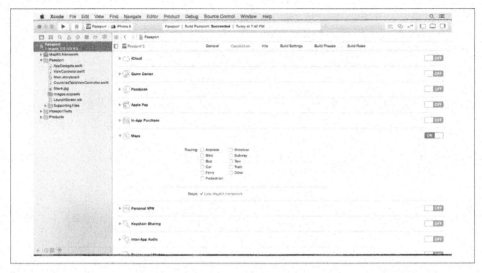

Figure 8-2. Capabilities tab

A new *MapKit.framework* item will appear in the Project Navigator. Next, select File→New→File from the top menu bar. Select Cocoa Touch Class and click Next.

Select UIViewController in the "Subclass of" drop-down menu and then name the class **MapViewController** (Figure 8-3). Verify the language is set to Swift and click Next. Save the file inside the Passport folder and click Create. A new *MapViewController.swift* file will be opened.

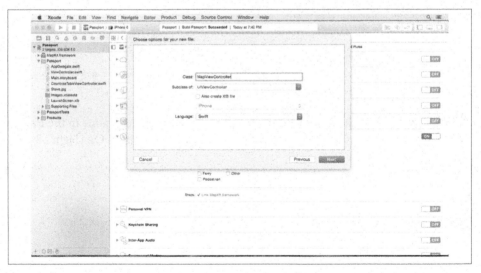

Figure 8-3. Naming class file

Highlight the green methods at the bottom of the file and delete them. Be sure not to remove the closing brace at the very bottom of the file. Delete the didReceiveMemory Warning method as well.

Open *Main.storyboard* (Figure 8-4). Verify the size class is "Any, Any." If it is not, click the size class link at the bottom, and a small pop-up box will appear. Select the middle box in the middle row (Figure 8-5).

Figure 8-4. Open Main.storyboard

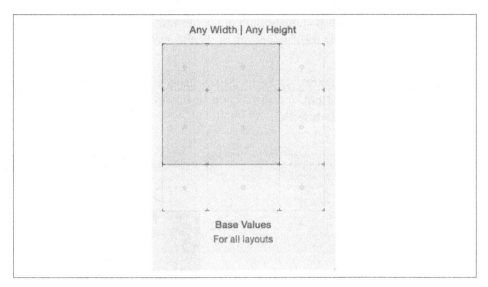

Figure 8-5. Grid

The interface will change size, but do not worry because the constraints are still in place. Hide the Project Navigator and the Document Outline. Open the Inspector. Then scroll to the right of the Table View Controller Scene (Figure 8-6).

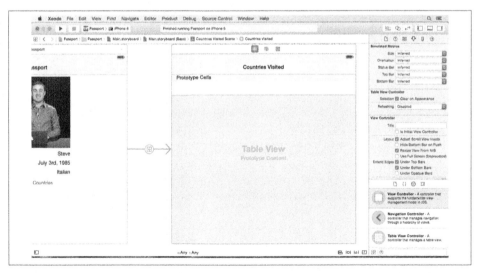

Figure 8-6. Countries Visited table view

In the Object Library, drag out a View Controller and place it to the right of the Table View Controller Scene. Then inside the Object Library, type **Map** and drag a Map View onto the new scene (Figure 8-7). Stretch the map until each edge snaps to the edge of the scene.

Select the Map View. From the top menu bar, select Editor→Pin→Leading Space to Superview. Select the Map View again and select Editor→Pin→Trailing Space to Superview. Select the Map View again and select Editor→Pin→Top Space to Superview. Select the Map View again and select Editor→Pin→Bottom Space to Superview. This will ensure the Map View fits the screen for any size device.

Clear the Object Library search box and type **BarButton**. Select the Bar Button Item from the Object Library and drag it to the upper-right corner of the Table View Controller Scene. Double-click the new Bar Button Item and type **Map**. Control-drag from the Map button to the new Map scene. A small pop-up box will appear. Select the show option (Figure 8-8).

A navigation bar will appear on top of the Map scene.

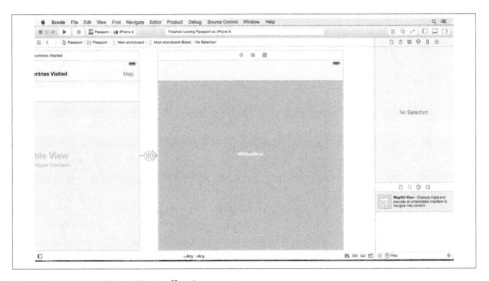

Figure 8-7. Map View Controller Scene

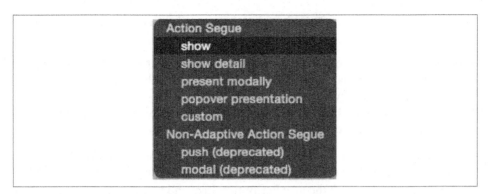

Figure 8-8. Action segue dialog

Click the blue MKMapView item inside the scene (Figure 8-9). Then Control-drag to the yellow circle at the top of the scene. This yellow circle represents the view controller for the scene.

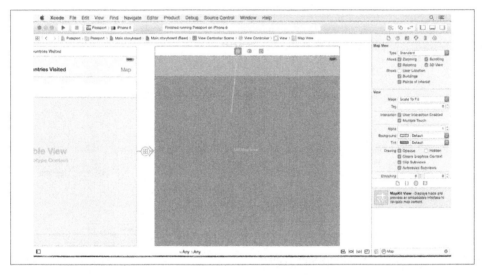

Figure 8-9. Connection

A small menu will appear; select the delegate option (Figure 8-10). This will ensure the *MapViewController.swift* file will receive delegate updates from the MKMapView.

Figure 8-10. Delegate pop-up menu

The storyboard is nearly complete, but you must connect the new Map scene to the *MapViewController.swift* file you created earlier. First, click the small yellow circle at the top of the scene. Next, open the Identity Inspector. The Identity Inspector manages the custom class for a scene. Select the third icon from the left on the top toolbar inside the Inspector to open the Identity Inspector. Inside the class input box, type **MapView Controller** (Figure 8-11). This ensures the connection of the *MapViewController.swift* file and your newly created scene.

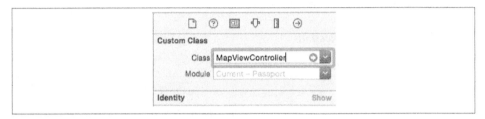

Figure 8-11. MapViewController class

Next, hide the Inspector and open the Assistant Editor. Click the Preview item at the top of the Assistant Editor and then select Automatic. Then Control-drag from the `MKMapView` to *MapViewController.swift* (Figure 8-12). A pop-up menu will appear (Figure 8-13).

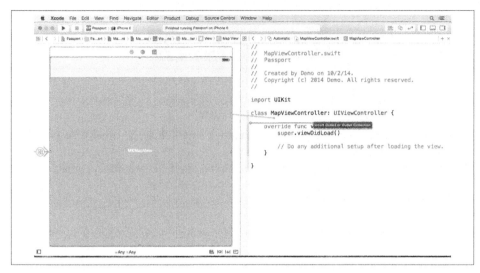

Figure 8-12. Blue line connection

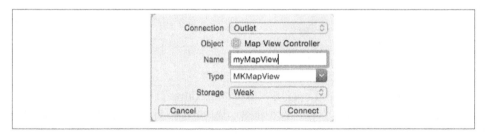

Figure 8-13. MKMapView connection dialog

Type **myMapView** into the Name input box. Then click Connect. An IBOutlet will be created. But there will be a few red lines and errors displayed as well. These errors are because the Map Kit framework has not been imported into the MapViewController class. To import Map Kit, just below the line that reads import UIKit, type **import Map Kit** (Figure 8-14).

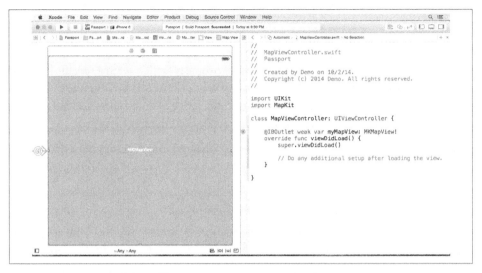

Figure 8-14. Imported Map Kit

The errors will be resolved, and the code warnings will be dismissed. The MapViewController will receive delegate updates whenever an event is triggered by the map. To receive these updates, the MapViewController must subscribe to the MKMapView Delegate protocol. To do this, add the bolded code:

```
class MapViewController: UIViewController, MKMapViewDelegate {
```

This will declare that the MapViewController is subscribed to the MKMapView Delegate protocol's list of events. Place your cursor in the viewDidLoad method under the line super.viewDidLoad().

Inside the viewDidLoad method, you will create four MKPointAnnotation objects. These objects will hold the position and title information for the pins placed on the map. Add the following code to the viewDidLoad() method:

```
let italy = MKPointAnnotation()
italy.coordinate = CLLocationCoordinate2DMake(41.8947400,12.4839000)
italy.title = "Rome, Italy"

let england = MKPointAnnotation()
england.coordinate = CLLocationCoordinate2DMake(51.5085300, -0.1257400)
england.title = "London, England"

let norway = MKPointAnnotation()
norway.coordinate = CLLocationCoordinate2DMake(59.914225, 10.75256)
norway.title = "Oslo, Norway"

let spain = MKPointAnnotation()
```

```
spain.coordinate = CLLocationCoordinate2DMake(40.41694, -3.70081)
spain.title = "Madrid, Spain"
```

This code creates the MKPointAnnotations. The first line sets a constant named italy to a new MKPointAnnotation. The coordinate property is then set to a specific location. The CLLocationCoordinate2DMake method takes the latitude and longitude of a location and creates a set of coordinates. Finally, the title property is set to the name of the city and country. This title will be displayed when the pin is tapped.

The four MKPointAnnotations must be added to the map, but first they need to be added to an array. Create an array holding the four new locations like this. Add this code just below the spain MKPointAnnotation:

```
let locations = [italy, england, norway, spain]
```

This creates a constant array named locations and adds the four MKPoint Annotations. These annotations can all be added to the map using the addAnnota tions() method provided by MKMapView. Add the following code just below the previous line:

```
myMapView.addAnnotations(locations)
```

This line will send a message to myMapView and tell it to add the italy, england, spain, and norway points to the map. However, there is still one more step to the process. All MKPointAnnotations must be paired with a MKPinAnnotationView. This matching takes place inside the mapView(_: viewForAnnotation:) method. Place your cursor just outside the closing brace of viewDidLoad and type the following:

```
func mapView(mapView: MKMapView!, viewForAnnotation annotation: MKAnnotation!)
-> MKAnnotationView! {

}
```

This method responds to the MKMapViewDelegate event triggered when an annotation is added to the map. This is where the matching between MKPointAnnotations and MKPinAnnotationViews takes place. Inside the new mapView(_: viewForAnnota tion:) method, add the following code (Figure 8-15):

```
func mapView(mapView: MKMapView!, viewForAnnotation annotation: MKAnnotation!)
-> MKAnnotationView! {

        var pin = MKPinAnnotationView(annotation: annotation,
         reuseIdentifier: "pinIdentifier")
        pin.canShowCallout = true

        return pin
}
```

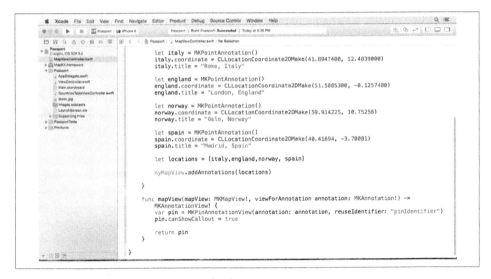

```
        let italy = MKPointAnnotation()
        italy.coordinate = CLLocationCoordinate2DMake(41.8947400, 12.4839000)
        italy.title = "Rome, Italy"

        let england = MKPointAnnotation()
        england.coordinate = CLLocationCoordinate2DMake(51.5085300, -0.1257400)
        england.title = "London, England"

        let norway = MKPointAnnotation()
        norway.coordinate = CLLocationCoordinate2DMake(59.914225, 10.75256)
        norway.title = "Oslo, Norway"

        let spain = MKPointAnnotation()
        spain.coordinate = CLLocationCoordinate2DMake(40.41694, -3.70081)
        spain.title = "Madrid, Spain"

        let locations = [italy,england,norway, spain]

        myMapView.addAnnotations(locations)

    }

    func mapView(mapView: MKMapView!, viewForAnnotation annotation: MKAnnotation!) ->
        MKAnnotationView! {
        var pin = MKPinAnnotationView(annotation: annotation, reuseIdentifier: "pinIdentifier")
        pin.canShowCallout = true

        return pin
    }

}
```

Figure 8-15. viewForAnnotation method

This method is called once for each annotation added to the map. The first line sets a variable named `pin` to a new `MKPinAnnotationView`. That `MKPinAnnotationView` is created, and the `annotation` property is set to the `annotation` parameter.

The current `MKPointAnnotation` is provided inside a parameter called `annotation`. This can be confusing; however, it is not uncommon to see the same word used twice to represent two different variables. It is important to realize the difference between the `annotation` property and the `annotation` parameter. The `annotation` property, available on `MKPinAnnotationView`, is used to position the pin on the map. The `annotation` parameter is the `MKPointAnnotation` currently being matched to an `MKPinAnnotationView` (i.e., `italy`, `england`, `spain`, or `norway`).

The `reuseIdentifier` for the newly created `MKPinAnnotationView` is set to **pinIdentifier**; this identifier is used to find and recycle `MKPinAnnotationViews` when there are large amounts of pins on a map. Finally, the new `MKPinAnnotationView`'s `canShowCallout` property is set to `true`. This enables the callout bubble to be shown when the pin is tapped on the map.

Place your cursor below the line `myMapView.addAnnotations(locations)` and then add the following lines of code:

```
var myRegion = MKCoordinateRegionMakeWithDistance(italy.coordinate,
5500000,5500000)

myMapView.setRegion(myRegion, animated: true)
```

The first line creates a variable named `myRegion` and sets it to a new `MKCoordinate`
`Region`. The `MKCoordinateRegion` is created using the `MKCoordinateRegionMakeWith`
`Distance()` method. This method take a point and creates a region around it, based on
the distance provided.

The second line sends a message to the map and tells it to set its region to the newly
created `myRegion`. The zoom is animated because of the `true` parameter. Run the application, but this time set the test device to iPhone 6 Plus (Figure 8-16).

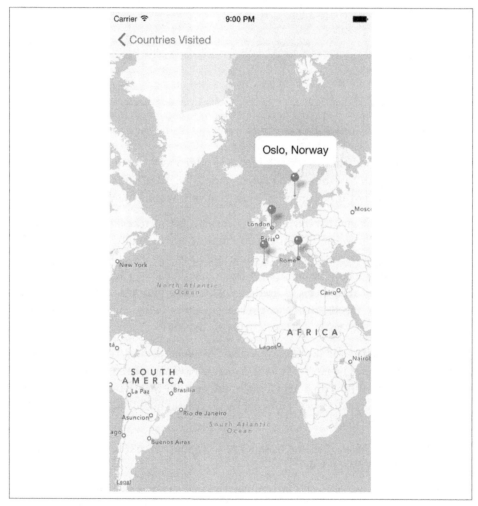

Figure 8-16. Completed on iPhone 6 Plus

The pins are now automatically shown when the app is launched. Stop the app and test
it on an iPad Air (Figure 8-17).

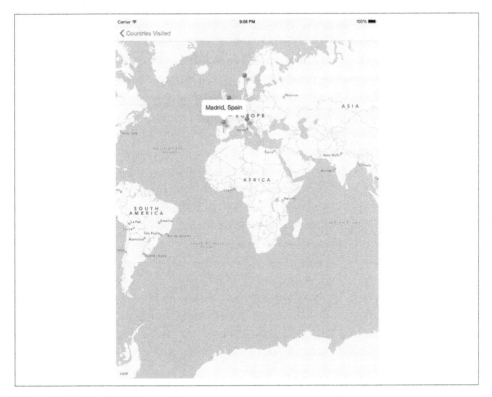

Figure 8-17. iPad Air

Notice the pins are placed in the center of the iPad's screen. Rotate the iPad, and the map view rotates as well.

Don't worry if you received an error, a warning, or your app did not run as expected. The best way to learn is to make mistakes. Practice makes perfect. A sample version of the project is available on AppSchool.com/book. Download it, compare it, and try, try again. Don't be afraid to start the exercise over and walk through it until you get it right.

CHAPTER 9

Camera, Photos, and Social Networks

In this chapter, you will learn how to incorporate camera functionality into your apps. You will also learn how to access photos and videos from the Photo Library. Finally, you will learn how to integrate your app with popular social networks like Facebook and Twitter. This chapter will teach you the most important pieces of the Swift language, so you can start building apps faster. These pieces were created by Apple to provide a quick and easy way to integrate the camera and connect to social networks.

UIImagePickerController

Apple provides a simple class to take and view photos or video. `UIImagePicker Controller`, shown in Figure 9-1, may look familiar because it is used in many iOS system-wide apps. `UIImagePickerController` can be configured to show the front or back camera's live image right inside your app. It can also be configured to display the Photo Library and allow users to select photos or videos.

`UIImagePickerController` is a simple interface that is presented modally above another view controller. A modal view controller is displayed above the current view controller, like a pop-up window. The modal view controller will slide up from the bottom of the screen and must be closed by the user when complete. Modal view controllers should only be used for temporary or short-term interactions.

Figure 9-1. UIImagePickerController

A `UIImagePickerController` object is created like any other object. Create a variable and call the initializer:

```
var imagePicker = UIImagePickerController()
```

Cameras

Before using the `UIImagePickerController`, it is important to detect if and what cameras are available on the device. In some cases, a device may have a camera, but it could be unavailable. Detect a camera on the device with the following example code:

```
if UIImagePickerController.isSourceTypeAvailable(.Camera) {
    //Camera is Available
}else{
        //Camera not Available
}
```

If a camera is available on the device, then you can set the `UIImagePickerController` to use that camera to take photos and videos. To set the `UIImagePickerController` to camera mode, set the `sourceType` property to `.Camera`:

```
imagePicker.sourceType = .Camera
```

Many iOS devices have multiple cameras, both front and rear. To check if there is a front or rear camera available, use the `isCameraDeviceAvailable` method. Provide the camera location to `isCameraDeviceAvailable`, and the method will return a `true` or `false` response:

```
if UIImagePickerController.isCameraDeviceAvailable(.Front) {
        //Front Camera Available
} else {
        //Front Camera Not Available
}

if UIImagePickerController.isCameraDeviceAvailable(.Rear) {
        //Rear Camera Available
} else {
        //Rear Camera Not Available
}
```

If there are no cameras available on the device, the `UIImagePickerController` can ask the user to pick a photo or video from the Photo Library. Set the `sourceType` property to `.PhotoLibrary` to show the Photo Library picker:

```
imagePicker.sourceType = .PhotoLibrary
```

Testing on the iOS Simulator can be limited at times since it will not have a camera. It is important to never assume a device will have a camera and always check using the provided methods. To properly test the camera functionality, you must run your app on an actual iOS device. Running your app on a device will be covered in depth in Chapter 10.

Media Types

The type of media can be set to photos, video, or both. By default, both photos and videos will be available. To change this, you must import the Mobile Core Services framework.

To add the Mobile Core Services framework to your project, click the project's name inside the Project Navigator. The project details will appear; scroll to the bottom and find the Linked Frameworks and Libraries section. Click the plus button in the bottom-left corner. Type **MobileCoreServices** into the search box, select *MobileCoreServices.framework*, and click Add.

The *MobileCoreServices.framework* file will be added to your Project Navigator. Then you must add the following to the top of your view controller:

```
import MobileCoreServices
```

This line will import the Mobile Core Services framework's classes into the view controller and make them available. There is a keyword for each media type:

kUTTypeImage

Photos and images

kUTTypeMovie

Movies and videos

Set the mediaTypes property with an array holding the appropriate values. For example:

```
imagePicker.mediaTypes = [kUTTypeImage]
//Only Images will be created or selected

imagePicker.mediaTypes = [kUTTypeMovie]
//Only Videos will be created or selected
```

Editing

Apple even provides a set of controls for scaling a photo or trimming a video. These are called *editing controls*. Set the allowsEditing property to true to enable them. For example:

```
imagePicker.allowsEditing = true
```

An editing screen will be added to the capture or selection workflow. You will be able to access both the edited and unedited media.

Delegates

UIImagePickerController provides delegate updates for typical user interaction. For example, a delegate update is sent when the user saves a new piece of media. To receive these updates, set the UIImagePickerController's delegate to the current view controller. Use the self keyword to represent the current view controller. For example:

```
imagePicker.delegate = self
```

Also, ensure the delegate view controller conforms to the UIImagePickerController Delegate protocol. You can conform to the protocol by adding the following code to your view controller. For example:

```
class ViewController: UIViewController, UIImagePickerControllerDelegate {
```

Since the UIImagePickerController inherits from UINavigatonController, its delegate must also conform to UINavigatonControllerDelegate protocol. This protocol provides updates for UINavigationController events like pushes and pops. Your view controller must conform to the protocol, but the methods are optional. To conform, add the following code to your view controller:

```
class ViewController: UIViewController, UIImagePickerControllerDelegate,
UINavigationControllerDelegate {
```

Working with Images

`UIImagePickerControllerDelegate` has two methods for dealing with media. The first method available is called `imagePickerController(_: didFinishPickingImage)`. This method will alert the delegate when an image has been taken by the camera or selected from the Photo Library. It will not be called if the user creates or selects a video. This method also provides a convenient `UIImage` parameter containing the newly formed image. To be alerted of this event, add the following code to your view controller:

```
func imagePickerController(picker: UIImagePickerController!,
  didFinishPickingImage image: UIImage!, editingInfo: [NSObject : AnyObject]!){
}
```

Working with Multiple Media Types

The second, and more advanced method, is `imagePickerController(_:, didFinish PickingMediaWithInfo _:)`. This method will alert the delegate when the user has created or selected a photo or video. If the `sourceType` is set to `.PhotoLibrary`, the method will be called after a photo or video has been selected. If the `sourceType` is set to `.Camera`, the method will be called after a photo or video has been taken and confirmed. The `info` parameter provides additional details about the new photo or video.

To be alerted for this event, add the following code to your view controller:

```
func imagePickerController(picker:UIImagePickerController,
  didFinishPickingMediaWithInfo info: [NSObject : AnyObject]){
                //media selected
}
```

The `info` parameter also includes a variable with its `mediaType`. It is very important to check the `mediaType` before accessing the new photo or video. Check the `mediaType` by accessing the `UIImagePickerControllerMediaType` key inside the `info` parameter:

```
var mediaType = info[UIImagePickerControllerMediaType]
```

The `info` dictionary parameter has many pieces of information about the newly created or selected content. The following keys will provide values describing the selected content:

`UIImagePickerControllerMediaType`
> Media type such as `kUTTypeImage` or `kUTTypeMovie`

`UIImagePickerControllerOriginalImage`
> Original uncropped image

`UIImagePickerControllerEditedImage`
> Edited image, only if `allowsEditing` is set to `true`

`UIImagePickerControllerCropRect`
> The cropping rectangle applied to the original image

`UIImagePickerControllerMediaURL`
> Path on local filesystem to video file (video only)

`UIImagePickerControllerReferenceURL`
> URL used with advanced video framework

`UIImagePickerControllerMediaMetadata`
> Photos only, dictionary full of metadata for image

All of these keys can be accessed for additional information about the media. The most popular keys are `UIImagePickerControllerMediaType`, `UIImagePickerControllerOriginalImage`, and `UIImagePickerControllerMediaURL`.

Once the `mediaType` has been recovered, run it through an `if` statement to detect if it is a video or a photo. For example:

```
var mediaType = info[UIImagePickerControllerMediaType! as NSString]

if  mediaType == kUTTypeImage as NSString {
        //photo
}else if mediaType == kUTTypeMovie {
        //video
}else {
        //error/missing
}
```

Images with didFinishPickingMediaWithInfo

If the `mediaType` is an image, the image will be provided directly inside the `info` parameter. The new image can be pulled out of the dictionary and placed directly into a `UIImage`. A `UIImage` is a class used for holding an image. `UIImages` are commonly passed to `UIImageViews`. `UIImageViews` are like picture frames; they hold an image and the image can be changed at any time. The `UIImageView` displays the `UIImage` on the user interface. The image is available with the `UIImagePickerControllerOriginalImage` key. For example:

```
var myImage = info[UIImagePickerControllerOriginalImage] as UIImage
```

Setting an image to a `UIImageView` is straightforward. Set the `UIImageView`'s `image` property to the `UIImage` provided by the `UIImagePickerControllerOriginalImage` key:

```
imageView.image = myImage
```

Video in didFinishPickingMediaWithInfo

If the `mediaType` is a video, the video will not be provided inside the dictionary. Instead, a path to the video file will be provided using the `UIImagePickerControllerMe diaURL` key. This process of using a path to the video instead of the actual video saves on memory and processing power. The path to the video can be passed to an `MPMovie PlayerViewController` and be played back on the user's screen. To access the video, add the following code to your view controller:

```
var videoPath = info[UIImagePickerControllerMediaURL as NSURL]
```

`MPMoviePlayerController` is a class dedicated to making video playback easy. The entire video playback process is handled for you. Provide the `MPMoviePlayer Controller` the path to a video, and it will play the video and display playback controls. The `MPMoviePlayerViewController` requires the Media Player framework.

To add the Media Player framework to your project, click the project's name inside the Project Navigator. The project details will appear; scroll to the bottom and find the Linked Frameworks and Libraries section. Click the plus button in the bottom-left corner. Type **MediaPlayer** into the search box, select *MediaPlayer.framework*, and click Add.

The *MediaPlayer.framework* will be added to your Project Navigator. Open the view controller and place your cursor at the top under the line `import UIKit`. Add the following:

```
import MediaPlayer
```

This line will import the Media Player framework's classes into the view controller and make them available. `MPMoviePlayerViewController` is included in this set of classes.

Next, create an `MPMoviePlayerViewController` like you would any other object. Then set its `contentURL` property:

```
var videoPath = info[UIImagePickerControllerMediaURL as NSURL]
var myMoviePlayerViewController = MPMoviePlayerViewController()
myMoviePlayerViewController.moviePlayer.contentURL = videoPath
```

Presenting UIImagePickerController

To present a new view controller, use the `presentViewController` method available in each `UIViewController`:

```
self.presentViewController(imagePicker, animated: true, completion: nil)
```

Integrating with Social Networks

Sharing to social networks has become a core feature in many a mobile app. However, integrating with each social network can be time consuming. Apple has created the Social framework to make sharing to social networks simple. Inside the Social framework is SLComposeViewController. This class provides the user with the ability to post to Twitter or Facebook. SLComposeViewController uses the Twitter and Facebook login information from the iOS Settings app. This means developers do not have to write code to authenticate with Twitter or Facebook. The interface allows the user to share text, links, and even images.

Before creating an SLComposeViewController, the Social framework must be imported into the project. Click the project's name in the Project Navigator; the project details will be shown. Scroll to the bottom next to Linked Frameworks and Libraries. Then click the plus button in the lower-left corner and type **Social** into the search box. Select *Social.framework* and click Add. The *Social.framework* file will be added to the Project Navigator. Finally, open the view controller file and place your cursor under the line import UIKit. Add the following code:

```
import Social
```

Setting the Social Network

This line will import the Social framework into the view controller and make SLCompo seViewController available in your code. A SLComposeViewController must have a serviceType provided when it is created. The serviceType property accepts two different options:

SLServiceTypeFacebook
: Facebook

SLServiceTypeTwitter
: Twitter

It is important to first verify that the desired service is available. To find out which service types are available on the device, use the isAvailableForServiceType(_:) method:

```
if (SLComposeViewController.isAvailableForServiceType(SLServiceTypeFacebook)) {
    //Facebook available
}
```

You can create the SLComposeViewController using the _(forServiceType:) method. This method creates an SLComposeViewController for the social network provided in the forServiceType parameter:

```
if (SLComposeViewController.isAvailableForServiceType(SLServiceTypeFacebook)) {
    //Facebook available
    var myComposeViewController = SLComposeViewController
```

```
                    (forServiceType: SLServiceTypeFacebook)
    }
```

Setting the Initial Text

You can also set the initial text for an SLComposeViewController. The initial text is a prewritten message that can be erased or shared by the user. To create the initial text, use the setInitialText(_:) method:

```
var myComposeViewController = SLComposeViewController
(forServiceType: SLServiceTypeFacebook)

myComposeViewController.setInitialText("I love this app!")
```

Adding Images

SLComposeViewControllers can also support images. To add an image to the user's post, use the addImage(_:) method. This method asks for a UIImage as a parameter and attaches it to the newly composed message:

```
myComposeViewController.addImage(myImage)
```

Adding URLs

A social media post would be helpless without a link. SLComposeViewController supports adding a URL to the message as well. To add a URL, use the addURL(_:) method. This method accepts an NSURL as a parameter. An NSURL is very similar to a string; however, it is specifically used for URLs and file paths. For example:

```
var myURL = NSURL(string: "http://www.google.com")
myComposeViewController.addURL(myURL)
```

Presenting SLComposeViewController

Finally, once the SLComposeViewController is created and configured, it is time to modally present it to the user. To present a view controller modally, use the present ViewController(_: animated: completion:) method. For example:

```
self.presentViewController(myComposeViewController,
animated: true, completion: nil)
```

The SLComposeViewController will be displayed, and the user can compose and then send their social network post. If a user is not logged in to the desired social network, iOS will prompt him to log in using the Settings app.

Now it is time to put your knowledge to the test. Keep up the momentum and build your very own Selfie app.

Exercise: A Selfie App

Throughout the remaining chapters of this book, you will build an app and submit it to the App Store. The app you will build is called *Selfie*. Selfie allows users to snap a photo using the camera and share it to Facebook (Figure 9-2). This app will be for iPhone only and will use the new UIImagePickerController lessons from this chapter.

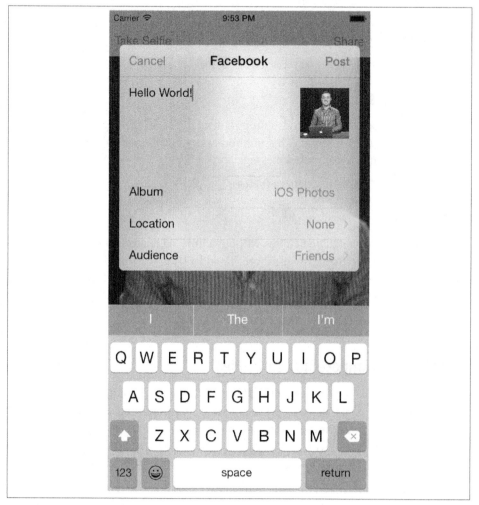

Figure 9-2. Selfie Facebook share

To begin, open Xcode from your Dock. Then select File→New Project. Select Single View Application and then click Next.

Name the product **Selfie** and set the Organization Name and Organization Identifier to your first and last name with no spaces (Figure 9-3). Verify that the Language is set to Swift and select iPhone from the Devices drop-down menu. Click Next. Save the project inside your Programming folder and click Create.

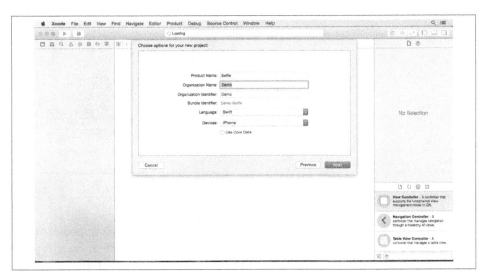

Figure 9-3. Product options

The project details will be displayed; under the Device Orientation section, deselect the Landscape Left and Landscape Right checkboxes (Figure 9-4).

Figure 9-4. Project details

Scroll to the bottom of the project details to the Linked Frameworks and Libraries section (Figure 9-5). Click the small plus button in the bottom-left corner. Type **So cial** into the search box, select the *Social.framework* file, and click Add. The framework will appear in the Project Navigator. Drag it into the Supporting Files folder if you want to hide it.

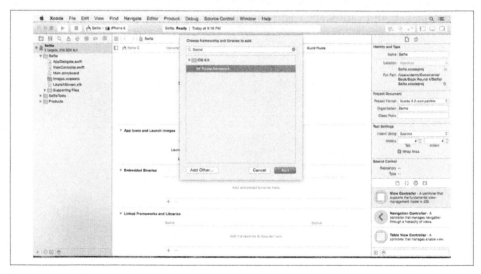

Figure 9-5. Libraries

Open the *Main.storyboard* file (Figure 9-6). Drag an Image View from the Object Library in the bottom right of your screen. Expand the Image View to cover the entire interface. Drag the Image View until it snaps with each edge of the interface. Select the Image View and open the Attributes Inspector. Change the mode to Aspect Fill.

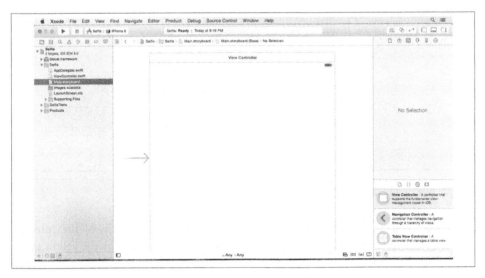

Figure 9-6. Blank storyboard

Next, select Editor→Pin→Leading Space to Superview. Then select the Image View again and click Editor→Pin→Trailing Space to Superview. Then select the Image View again and click Editor→Pin→Top Space to Superview. Finally, select the Image View again and click Editor→Pin→Bottom Space to Superview. This will ensure that the Image View fits the screen for any iPhone size (Figure 9-7).

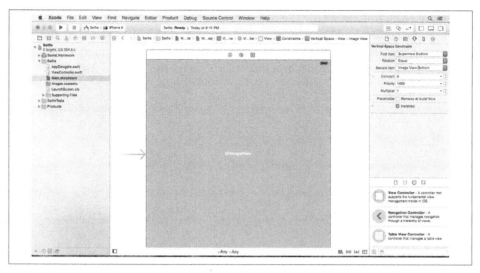

Figure 9-7. Add constraints

Next, you will add a navigation bar and two buttons to the top of the interface (Figure 9-8). Click the white bar at the top of the scene and then click the yellow circle. Next, from the top menu bar, select Editor→Embed In→Navigation Controller. A navigation bar will appear in the interface. Double-click the middle of the navigation bar and type **Selfie**.

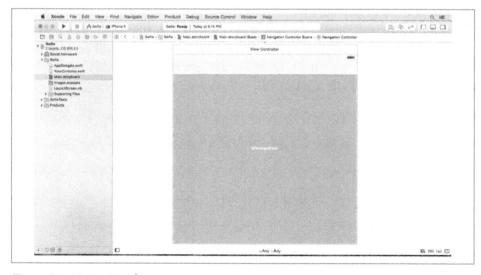

Figure 9-8. Navigation bar

Scroll back to the main view controller and drag a Bar Button Item from the Object Library. Release the Bar Button Item on the left side of the navigation bar. Double-click the Bar Button Item and change the name to **Take Selfie**. Pull out another Bar Button Item from the Object Library and release the Bar Button Item on the right side of the navigation bar. Double-click the Bar Button Item and change the name to **Share** (Figure 9-9).

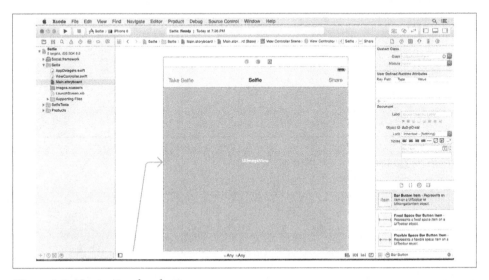

Figure 9-9. Navigation bar buttons

Now that each interface element has been positioned on the screen, it is time to connect the elements to the *ViewController.swift* file. Open the Assistant Editor; then hide the Inspector and Document Outline. Remove the viewDidLoad and didReceiveMemory Warning methods.

Then, while holding the Control button, click and drag from the Image View to the Assistant Editor. Release your drag just under the line that reads class ViewController: UIViewController (Figure 9-10). A small pop-up box will appear (Figure 9-11).

Figure 9-10. Image View connection

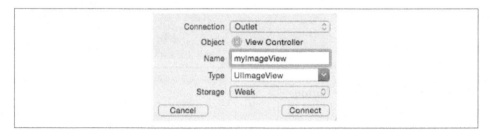

Figure 9-11. Pop-up

Verify the Outlet option is selected in the Connection drop-down menu. Name the outlet **myImageView** and click Connect.

While holding Control, drag from the Take Selfie button to the *ViewController.swift* file. Release the drag just below the line that starts with **@IBOutlet** (Figure 9-12). A small pop-up box will appear (Figure 9-13).

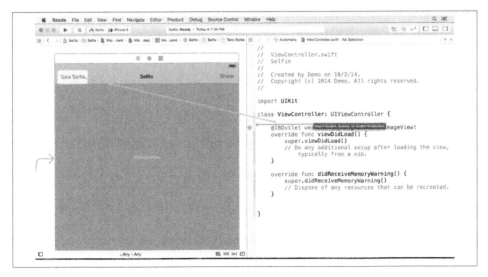

Figure 9-12. Take Selfie connection

Figure 9-13. Pop-up

Change the Connection type to Action, name it **selfieTapped**, and then click Connect. A selfieTapped method will automatically be created inside the *ViewController.swift* file.

Then Control-drag from the Share button to *ViewController.swift* file. Release the drag just below the line that starts with @IBOutlet (Figure 9-14). A small pop-up box will appear (Figure 9-15).

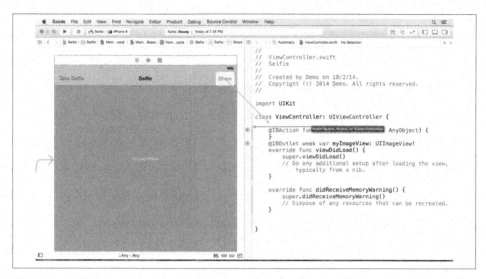

Figure 9-14. Share connection

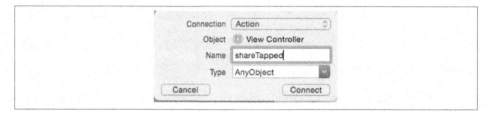

Figure 9-15. Po-up

Set the Connection type to Action. Set the name to **shareTapped** and click Connect. A **shareTapped** method will automatically be created inside the *ViewController.swift* file.

The interface elements are now connected to the controller. Hide the Assistant Editor and open the *ViewController.swift* file.

Add the following code to the **selfieTapped** method:

```
@IBAction func selfieTapped(sender: AnyObject){
        var imagePicker = UIImagePickerController()
        imagePicker.delegate = self

        self.presentViewController(imagePicker, animated: true, completion: nil)
}
```

The first line of code creates a new **UIImagePickerController** and sets it to the **image Picker** variable. The next line sets the **imagePicker**'s **delegate** property to the current view controller, also known as self. Finally, the last line presents the imagePicker modally, sliding it up from the bottom of the screen, and it animates the transition.

This new method has an error. The imagePicker.delegate line is the problem. Click the red dot, and the error message says:

Type "ViewController" does not conform to protocol 'UIImagePickerControllerDelegate

This is Xcode letting you know the ViewController instance must conform to the UIImagePickerControllerDelegate protocol. Remember, the delegate must conform to both UIImagePickerControllerDelegate and UINavigationControllerDelegate. Add the bolded code to the top of *ViewController.swift*:

```
class ViewController: UIViewController, UIImagePickerControllerDelegate
, UINavigationControllerDelegate {
```

Press Command+B on your keyboard to rebuild the project. Rebuilding the project will compile and analyze all of the lines of code, but does not start the simulator. This can be a helpful tool when fixing issues.

Then place your cursor below the line imagePicker.delegate = self and add the following code:

```
if UIImagePickerController.isSourceTypeAvailable(.Camera) {

} else {

}
```

The if statement will check and see if a camera is available on the device. If so, the top portion will execute; if not, the bottom section will execute. Add the following lines of code to the top portion of the if statement:

```
if UIImagePickerController.isSourceTypeAvailable(.Camera) {

        imagePicker.sourceType = .Camera

        if (UIImagePickerController.isCameraDeviceAvailable(.Front)) {
                imagePicker.cameraDevice = .Front
        } else {
                imagePicker.cameraDevice = .Rear
        }

}
```

The first line inside the top portion sets the imagePicker's sourceType property to .Camera. The next line is an if statement checking if a front camera is available. If so, the imagePicker's cameraDevice property is set to .Front. This will enable the front camera as the default camera. If a front camera is not available, the rear camera will be used.

Add the following line of code to the bottom portion of the `isSourceTypeAvailable` if statement:

```
} else {
        imagePicker.sourceType = .PhotoLibrary
}
```

The bottom portion of the `if` statement will be executed if there is not a camera available. In this case, the Photo Library should be shown. The line of code above sets the `sour ceType` property to `.PhotoLibrary` (Figure 9-16). This ensures that the Photo Library will be shown if no camera is available.

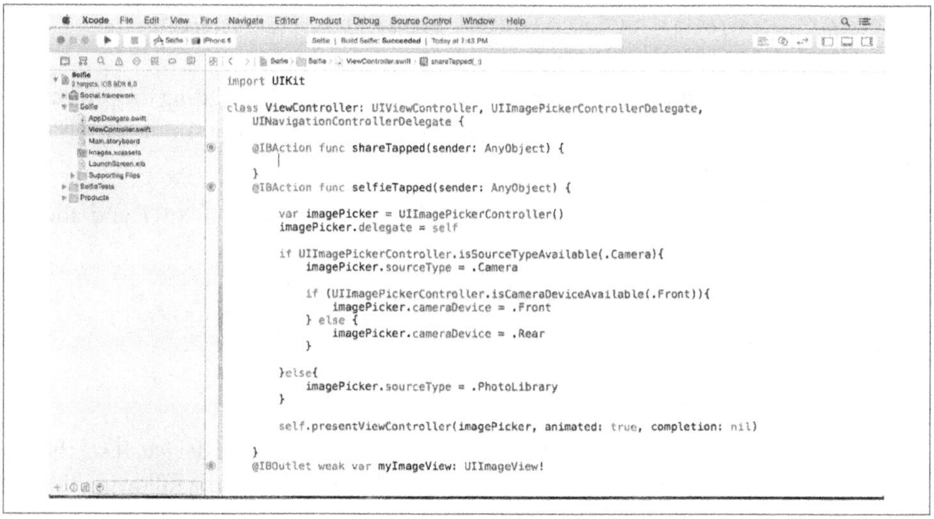

Figure 9-16. Updated code

Next, add the `didFinishPickingImage` delegate method. Add the following method below `selfieTapped`:

```
func imagePickerController(picker: UIImagePickerController!,
didFinishPickingImage image: UIImage!, editingInfo: [NSObject : AnyObject]!){

}
```

This method will be called when the user has taken a photo or has selected a photo from the Photo Library. The method has two parameters: the first is the `UIImagePicker Controller`, provided for convenience, and the second parameter is a `UIImage` named `image`. The `image` parameter contains the image selected or created by the user. Add the following code to *ViewController.swift*:

```
func imagePickerController(picker: UIImagePickerController!,
didFinishPickingImage image: UIImage!, editingInfo: [NSObject : AnyObject]!){
```

```
myImageView.image = image
self.dismissViewControllerAnimated(true, completion: nil)

}
```

The first line takes the `image` parameter and displays it inside `myImageView`. The next line hides the `imagePicker` and animates the transition.

Next, place your cursor below the `import UIKit` line and add the following:

```
import Social
```

This will import *Social.framework* into *ViewController.swift* . Place your cursor inside the new `shareTapped` method. This method will be called each time the Share button is tapped. Two things must happen inside this method: the image must be added, and the Facebook post dialog must be displayed.

Add the following code to `shareTapped( )`:

```
var social = SLComposeViewController(forServiceType: SLServiceTypeFacebook)
social.addImage(myImageView.image)

self.presentViewController(social, animated: true, completion: nil)
```

The first line creates an `SLComposeViewController` and sets the `serviceType` property to Facebook. Then the `myImageView` image is added to the Facebook post. Finally, the `SLComposeViewController` is displayed, and the transition is animated.

Build and run the project. Select a photo and tap Share. An alert will be displayed stating that the iOS Simulator does not have a Facebook account associated with it. Click the Settings option and then add a Facebook account. Once this is done, stop the iOS Simulator and relaunch the app (Figure 9-17).

Figure 9-17. iOS Simulator

Don't worry if you received an error, a warning, or your app did not run as expected. The best way to learn is to make mistakes. Practice makes perfect. A sample version of the project is available on AppSchool.com/book. Download it, compare it, and try, try again. Don't be afraid to start the exercise over and walk through it until you get it right.

CHAPTER 10
Running on a Device

In this chapter, you will learn how to run your newly developed apps on a device. You will also walk through how to create certificates, register your device for testing, and set up your App IDs and provisioning profiles. This chapter will combine the lecture and the exercise section; be sure to have Xcode open as you read.

Testing your apps on your own iOS device requires a registered Apple Developer account. A registered Apple Developer account is also required to release your app to the App Store. The Apple Developer Program provides developers with early release access to new versions of iOS and OSX. Registered Apple Developers are eligible to review sessions from WWDC. WWDC is Apple's *Worldwide Developer Conference* held every year in San Francisco. WWDC is used as a launching point for new Apple products and software. Apple Developers receive their own private telephone support number. Registering as an Apple Developer costs $99 per year. This is the best investment you can make toward learning to develop apps.

The rest of the content inside this book will require an Apple Developer Program account. You can sign up at *http://developer.apple.com/programs/ios*.

If you are a college student, Apple provides a free Apple Developer Program called iOS Developer University Program. More details can be found at *http://developer.apple.com/programs/ios/university*.

Your Apple Developer Program account can be registered to your legal name or your legal business entity. Registering under your legal name is known as an individual account. Registering under your legal business entity requires a D-U-N-S number and the proper legal documents to verify your business. A D-U-N-S number is an unique identifier for your business; you can learn more at *https://developer.apple.com/support/ios/D-U-N-S.php*. In most cases, it is easier to just register as an individual and transition the account to a business account when needed. For more information, visit *https:// developer.apple.com/programs/*.

Once you have registered with the Apple Developer Program, you will receive access to the *Member Center*. The Member Center is the hub for all Apple Developer tools and updates. You can log in to the Member Center at *https://developer.apple.com/member center/*. Inside the Member Center is a section called *Certifications, Identifiers, and Profiles*. This section is commonly known as the *Provisioning Portal*. This portal will control the devices and profiles used in your development.

Open your browser to *http://developer.apple.com* (Figure 10-1).

Figure 10-1. developer.apple.com

Click the Member Center link in the upper right and sign in with your Apple Developer Account (Figure 10-2).

Figure 10-2. Developer Portal

Click the link that says "Certifications, Identifiers, and Profiles." Then click the Certificates link.

The Provisioning Portal has four main sections. Bookmark this site in your web browser, since it will be used fairly often.

Certificates

The first section is named *Certificates*. Certificates are used to verify your identity when building an app. A unique certificate is created and is used as your signature. This limits outsiders from submitting apps to the App Store without your permission.

Open the Certificates section, and you will see a silver portal (Figure 10-3). On the left side, each section is outlined in the sidebar. The Pending section is reserved for certificates that are currently being processed. Development certificates are used for local development on your own computer. Finally, Production certificates are used for the App Store.

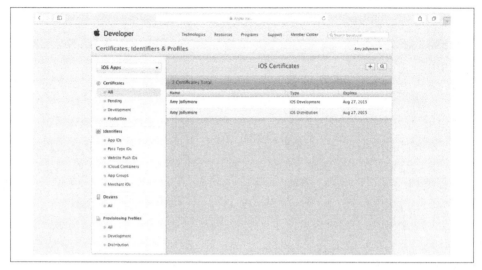

Figure 10-3. Certificates

Click the plus button in the upper-right corner. Select iOS App Development and then Continue. A wizard will appear asking you to select which type of certificate you would like to create (Figure 10-4). Click the iOS App Development box and click Continue. The wizard will now ask you to create a Certificate Signing Request (CSR). The CSR will be used as one of the ingredients for creating your certificate.

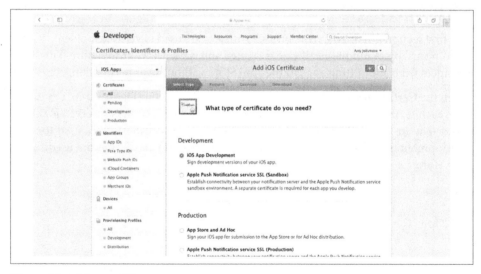

Figure 10-4. New certificate

To create a CSR, open the Keychain Access application on your Mac. Click the Spotlight search icon in the top right of your screen. Type in **Keychain Access** and select the Top Hit. Keychain Access will launch and show a list of all the certificates currently on your computer. Click Keychain Access in the top menu bar and then select Certificate Assistant→Request a Certificate From a Certificate Authority (Figure 10-5).

Figure 10-5. Keychain Access App

A wizard will appear on the screen (Figure 10-6). Fill out the email and common name fields, but leave the CA Email address field empty. Finally, check "Saved to disk" and click Continue. Choose where to save the file and click Save. Go back to the Provisioning Portal in your web browser.

Figure 10-6. Wizard

Once you have created a CSR, click the Continue button on the Provisioning Portal wizard (Figure 10-7). The Provisioning Portal will then ask you to upload the CSR file. Click the Choose File button and then browse to the *.certSigningRequest* file (Figure 10-8).

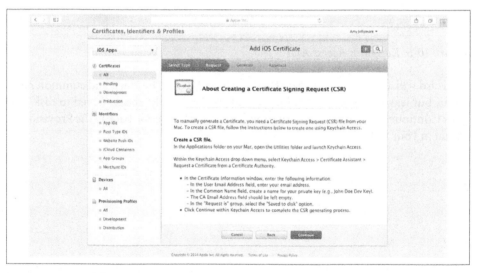

Figure 10-7. Web browser

Figure 10-8. CSR

Then click Generate, and the wizard will begin to create the certificate. Once the certificate is ready, a Download button will appear (Figure 10-9). Download the certificate and open your Downloads folder in Finder. Double-click the new *ios_development.cer* file to add it to your keychain.

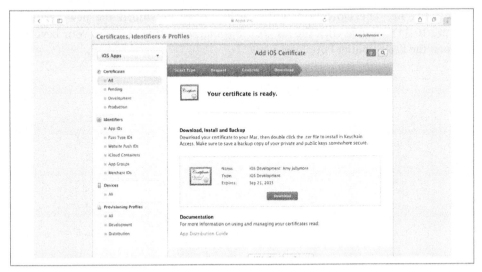

Figure 10-9. Download certificate

Reopen your web browser and click All under Certificates on the left side. A list of all your new certificates will be shown. A second certificate, for the App Store, must also be created. Click the plus button in the upper-right corner again. Choose "App Store and Ad Hoc" and then click Continue (Figure 10-10). The CSR creation screen will be shown, but you will use the CSR from last time. Click Continue.

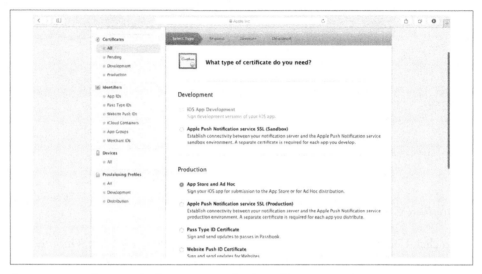

Figure 10-10. Choosing the "App Store and Ad Hoc" option

Click the Choose File button and select the *.certSigningRequest* created previously. Then click Generate. The Download button will appear; download the new certificate (Figure 10-11). Double-click the *ios_distribution.cer* file to add it into your keychain. Reopen the Provisioning Portal website.

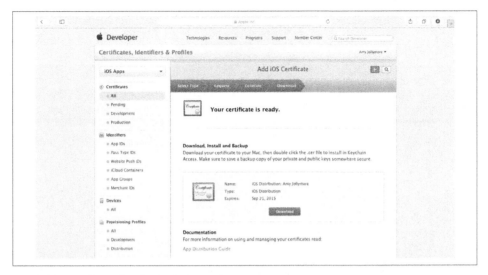

Figure 10-11. Download certificate

Identifiers

Below the Certificates section is another section called *Identifiers*. The Identifiers section is where the App IDs are managed. In the same way that each citizen of the United States has his or her own unique Social Security number, every app in the App Store has its own unique App ID.

To create an App ID, select App IDs from the sidebar and then click the plus button in the upper right-hand corner of the screen. The create App ID screen will be presented (Figure 10-12). Name your App ID **Selfie** without the quotes. Leave the App ID Prefix as is and select Explicit App ID. The Bundle ID is written using a reverse-domain style, similar to entering a web address into a web browser, except in reverse. You must come up with your own unique Bundle ID. Do not use the Bundle ID shown in the examples or screenshots, as they will not work. Enter your own Bundle ID into the Bundle ID input box. Be sure to use the following format: *com.domain.app* (for example, *com.john-smith.selfieapp*).

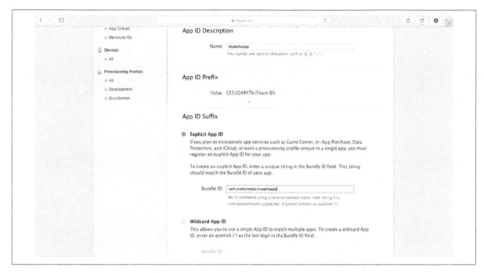

Figure 10-12. Register App ID

This Bundle ID will be entered into Xcode and matched when the app is submitted to the App Store. Finally, the App Services section is where you can enable additional services for your application. Click Continue. You will be asked to confirm your App ID; click Submit if everything is correct. Your App ID and Bundle ID have been created (Figure 10-13).

Figure 10-13. Confirmed App ID

Devices

You cannot run your app for testing on just any device. The devices used for testing and development must be declared with Apple. Developers are allowed to register up to 100 devices per year. If a device is removed, the slot is not reopened. The Devices section holds all the devices enabled for an Apple Developer Account. Devices are tracked using a unique serial number called a *UDID* attached to each device.

Click the All link under Devices and then click the plus button in the upper-right corner.

To register a device, you will need its UDID (Figure 10-14). To gather the UDID for a device, connect the device to a Mac running Xcode. When the device is connected, open Xcode and select Window→Devices from the top menu bar. The Devices window will appear; select the iOS device from the left sidebar. The iOS device will prompt you to Trust This Computer; tap Trust on your iOS device. The UDID will appear in the device details next to the word "Identifier." Copy it to your clipboard and reopen the Provisioning Portal.

Paste the identifier inside the UDID input box and give the device a name (Figure 10-14). Then click Continue.

Figure 10-14. Register Device

Profiles

Once your devices are activated for development and are added to the Devices section, you are ready to create a provisioning profile. A *provisioning profile* is a small file that specifies which devices can run your app. Provisioning profiles commonly list a set of test devices or beta tester's devices. The provisioning profile is added into Xcode, and the app checks to make sure the device running the app is authorized. Provisioning profiles are used for local development and for the App Store. However, the App Store provisioning profiles are not limited to a specific set of devices.

Click the All link under Provisioning Profiles. Then click the plus button in the upper-right corner.

Select iOS App Development and click Continue (Figure 10-15). Development is used for working and building your application on your computer. Distribution is reserved for sending your app to the App Store or a group of beta testers.

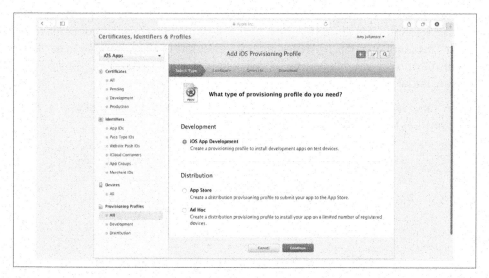

Figure 10-15. Select type

Next, select the Selfie App ID from the drop-down menu and then click Continue (Figure 10-16). You are asked to specify the certificate to use with this provisioning profile. In most cases, you will only have one certificate available. Select your certificate and click Continue.

Figure 10-16. Select App ID

Next, a list of the authorized devices for your developer account will be presented (Figure 10-17). Select the devices you would like to use to test Selfie.

Figure 10-17. Devices

Finally, name the profile using the format *projectNameDev* or *projectNameAppStore* (Figure 10-18). Setting the name to this format will make finding the provisioning profile in Xcode much easier. Name the profile **MySelfieAppDev**. Click Generate and download the profile.

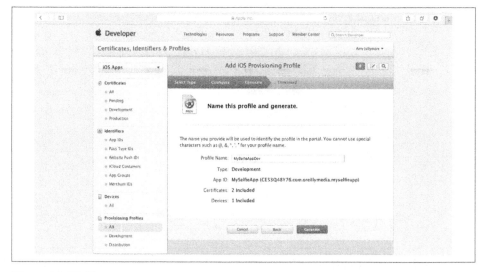

Figure 10-18. Name

Reopen the provisioning profile and click the All link in the Provisioning Profile section again. Then click the plus button in the upper-right corner.

Select App Store and click Continue. Select the Selfie App ID from the drop-down. Click Continue. Select the certificate and click Continue. Name the profile `SelfieAppStore` and then click Generate.

Download the profile and open your Downloads folder to the newly created provisioning profiles. They will be named *MySelfieAppDev.mobileprovision* and *MySelfieApp-Store.mobileprovision* (Figure 10-19). With the Downloads folder open, double-click each provisioning profile to add it to Xcode. Once the provisioning profiles are added to Xcode, you must set them inside the project.

Figure 10-19. Downloads

Open the Xcode project and select the project name inside the Project Navigator. The project details will be displayed inside the Editor. From the Team drop-down menu, select Add an Account. Enter your Apple Developer Program login and password; then click Add (Figure 10-20).

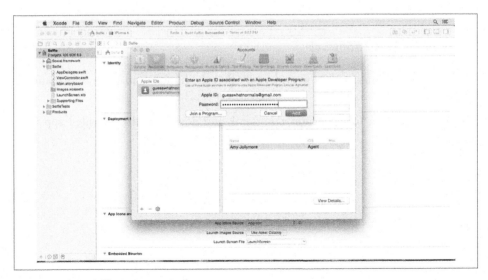

Figure 10-20. Add account window

Close the Accounts dialog and return to the project details. Click the Info tab at the top and clear the Bundle Identifier field. Then set the Bundle Identifier to the reverse-domain name entered when creating the App ID (for example, *com.johnsmith.selfieapp*).

Then select Build Settings and scroll down to the Code Signing section. Under Code Signing Identity, go to Debug and select iPhone Developer: YOUR NAME. Verify that the Any iOS SDK row below is the same. Under Release, select iPhone Distribution: YOUR NAME. Verify that the Any iOS SDK line is the same (Figure 10-21).

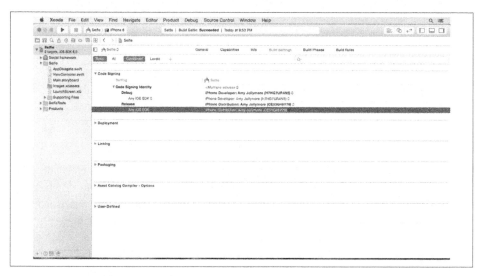

Figure 10-21. Build Settings tab

Click the General tab at the top and verify that the bundle and team information is correct.

Open your browser to AppSchool.com/book and download the provided app icons (Figure 10-22).

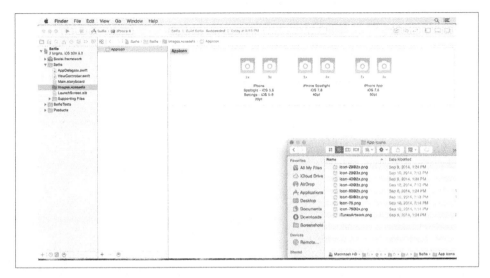

Figure 10-22. App icons

Open Finder to the new files. Open Xcode alongside the Finder window. Select *Images.xcassets* inside of the Project Navigator.

The application is now ready to run on a device. Connect your iOS device to your Mac and then click the iOS Simulator drop-down menu at the top of Xcode. Select your iOS device from the top of the menu and click the Play button.

You may see an alert from Xcode that reads "process launch failed: Security." This is simply a first-time warning. Tap the app on your device and select Trust from the App Developer prompt. The app will launch and ask for permission to use the camera. Use the app and share a selfie to Facebook. Then tap the home button to verify the new app icon is shown on the Home Screen. Congratulations! You are now running your own apps on a device.

Don't worry if you received an error, a warning, or your app did not run as expected. The best way to learn is to make mistakes. Practice makes perfect. A sample version of the project is available on AppSchool.com/book. Download it, compare it, and try, try again. Don't be afraid to start the exercise over and walk through it until you get it right.

CHAPTER 11

Submitting to the App Store

In this chapter, you will learn how to submit an app to the App Store. You will also learn how to use iTunes Connect, Apple's App Store management software (Figure 11-1). These lessons will give you the skills to submit your apps to the App Store. This chapter will walk you through iTunes Connect, so have your Mac nearby.

This app will be submitted to the App Store for educational purposes only. It is not possible to guarantee approval into the App Store. Be sure to use a unique app name and bundle ID while submitting this app.

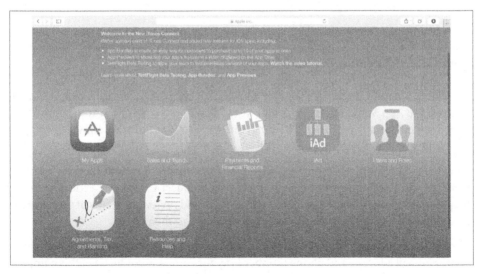

Figure 11-1. iTunes Connect

iTunes Connect is a website used to manage apps for the App Store. This is where all marketing, reporting, and contract details are entered. You can log in to iTunes Connect using your Apple Developer ID at *http://itunesconnect.apple.com*. iTunes Connect offers a companion app called *iTunes Connect Mobile* available on the App Store.

Agreements, Tax, and Banking

Before an app can be submitted to the App Store, you must first complete the "Agreements, Tax, and Banking" section (Figure 11-2). This section manages the contracts between Apple and the developer. It records the developer's banking information for payment.

Figure 11-2. Agreements, Tax, and Banking

By default, the iOS Developer Program allows all developers to release free apps worldwide on the App Store. However, if you would like to sell your apps on the App Store, a separate contract is required. The iOS Paid Applications contract allows developers to sell their app on the App Store.

To agree to the additional contract, click the "Agreements, Tax, and Banking" section from the iTunes Connect homepage. Inside the Request Contracts section, click the Request button on the Paid Applications line. Read and review the terms of the contract; then decide if you agree. If you agree, click Submit and then Done.

Click the Setup Contact Info button to create a company contact. Enter the full name, address, email address, and phone number for your company contact. Set this company contact to the "Senior Management, Financial, Technical, Legal, and Marketing" sections and then click Done.

Click the Setup Bank Info button to add your banking information. Click Add Bank Account and enter your country. Then enter the ABA routing number for your bank. If you do not know this information, click the lookup tool below. Finally, select the bank and enter your bank account number. Your gross earnings minus any returns will be direct-deposited to this bank account each month.

Finally, click the "Setup Banking and Tax Info" button and then click U.S. Tax forms. Enter your legal name and legal entity if this is a business account. Select the type of beneficial owner. Consult with your accountant if you are an exempt payee. Provide your legal address and name. Then provide your Social Security number or EIN in the Taxpayer Identification Number field. Carefully read and review the certification section. You will be unable to change this information once it is submitted. Be sure to verify that the information provided is correct before proceeding.

Now that the "Agreements, Tax, and Banking" section is complete, it is time to create the app listing for the App Store. The app listing holds all the marketing information for an app, including the app name, app description, app icon, keywords, screenshots, and more.

Create App Listing

The My Apps section manages app listings. From the iTunes Connect home screen, click My Apps. Click the plus button in the upper left, followed by New iOS App. The first screen shown will ask for some basic details about the app (Figure 11-3):

Name
    Spell this exactly as you would like to it appear on the App Store.

Version
    Enter the app version number here, typically 1.0 for a new app.

Primary Language
    This will be used for the app listing language.

Bundle ID
    Select an available App ID from the drop-down menu. This cannot be undone once the app listing is created.

SKU
    This can be anything you like; these are used to identify your apps for your own records.

Figure 11-3. New iOS app

Each version of the app will have its own specific App Store data. Most of the information will not be editable once the app has been approved. A new version of the app will be required to make changes to the app listing after it is approved.

Enter your own app name; make sure it is *not* Selfie. The App Store will not allow apps with the exact same name to be posted. One example name might be something like:

Selfie - Take and Share Selfie Photos

For the SKU number, enter a unique code to identify your app. This can be your first and last name pushed together with a number after it. For example:

JOHNSMITH001

Then select the Selfie Bundle ID created in the previous chapter from the drop-down menu. Click Continue.

Version Information

Next, the app listing page will appear. Scroll down, and you will the notice that the first section is called Version Information (Figure 11-4). The version information is specific to each version of your app. This means most information can only be changed when the app is updated.

Figure 11-4. Version Information section

The Version Information section collects the following information:

App Name
App name as it should appear in the App Store.

Description
This is a where you provide details and an explanation of why users should download your app.

Keywords
These keywords are used to help users find your app via search on the App Store.

Support URL
A website where users can go to file issues and provide feedback.

Marketing URL
Optional website providing more information about the app.

Privacy Policy URL
Optional website stating the app's privacy policy. This is required for apps with autorenewing subscriptions and apps for kids.

Keywords

The keywords listed will be used to help users find your app via search on the App Store. Keywords should be separated by a comma, with no spaces. The keyword input is limited to 100 characters total, including commas. These keywords cannot use names of other apps or brand names. Good keywords are descriptive of the app and what problem it solves. For example:

```
photos,image,snapshot,pictures,photograph,text,label,portrait
```

Enter your own keywords to the list and put them into the keyword input box.

Support URL

The support URL should be a place where users can go to submit questions and troubleshoot problems. It helps to have a website with a contact form or support email address listed. You can create a free website at *http://www.tumblr.com*.

Enter a support URL into the Support URL input box.

Description

The description should provide a brief outline of the app's features and how the app works. Write your own custom description here; review similar apps' descriptions to get a better idea of what is working. Here is the description for a popular photo-sharing app, Instagram:

> Over 200 million users love Instagram! It's a simple way to capture and share the world's moments on your iPhone. Customize your photos and videos with one of several gorgeous and custom-built filter effects. Transform everyday moments into works of art you'll want to share with friends and family.
>
> Share your photos and videos with friends and followers in a photo feed, or send posts directly to your friends.
> Follow what your friends post with the click of a single button. Every time you open up Instagram, you'll see new photos and videos from your closest friends and creative people from around the world. Features
> • 100% free custom designed filters: XPro-II, Earlybird, Rise, Amaro, Hudson, Lo-fi, Sutro, Toaster, Brannan, Inkwell, Walden, Hefe, Nashville, 1977, and others.
> • Video recording with breathtaking cinematic stabilization.
> • Linear and Radial Tilt-Shift blur effects for extra depth of field
> • Instant sharing to Facebook, Twitter, Flickr, Tumblr and Foursquare
> • Unlimited uploads
> • Send photos and videos directly to friends
> • Interact with friends through giving & receiving likes and comments
> • Full iPhone 4 front & back camera support
> • And much much more…

Enter your own app description and make sure it highlights the core features of the app. *Why is this app helpful? What does it do? Who is it for?*

Screenshots

The screenshots are arguably the most important piece of the marketing for your app (Figure 11-5). Studies have shown that most iOS users scroll directly to the screenshots to determine if they will download an app. Your screenshots should be bright, colorful, and engaging. At least one screenshot must be provided for 4.7-inch, 5.5-inch, 4-inch, and 3.5-inch formats. If an app is set to Universal, iPad screenshots are also required. If an app is set to iPad-only, then no iPhone-sized screenshots will be required.

Figure 11-5. Screenshots

To create a screenshot in the iOS Simulator, launch an app and press Command+S and a screenshot will be placed on the desktop.

Go through and take screenshots for an iPhone 4s, iPhone 5s, iPhone 6, and iPhone 6 Plus. Then go back to iTunes Connect.

Verify that 4.7-inch is selected, and from the desktop, drag the iPhone 6 screenshots into the iTunes Connect page. Once all the screenshots are uploaded, you can drag them left and right to place them in a particular order. The first screenshot is showcased in the app search in the App Store.

Select 5.5-inch and drag in the iPhone 6 Plus screenshots, select 4-inch and drag in the iPhone 5s screenshots, and select 3.5-inch and drag in the iPhone 4s screenshots.

Once this is complete, click Save in the upper-right corner of iTunes Connect.

General App Information

The next section, titled General App Information, collects the following information (Figure 11-6):

App Icon
> App icon used for App Store listing. Provide a 1024x1024 px image in JPG, TIFF, or PNG format. No transparency allowed. Do not round corners.

Category
> Primary and secondary category best suited for your app.

Rating
> Select the appropriate maturity level for your app.

Trade Rep Info
> This App Store contact information is used in the Korean App Store.

Routing App Coverage File
> Optional, used to specify a geographic region supported by the app.

Version Number
> Identifier for each version, follow pattern 1.0, 1.1, 1.2, etc.

Copyright
> Year and person or entity that owns the rights to the app.

License Agreement
> By default, the standard End User License Agreement will be applied to your app. If you want to change this, click the Edit button next to License Agreement at the bottom of the app listing.

Figure 11-6. General App Information

Tips

There are a few key tips and tricks to remember when creating marketing content:

1. Put as much effort into the App Store marketing as you did the development of your app.

2. Apps with engaging and compelling app icons and screenshots sell more than average-looking apps.

3. Check the Top Charts for examples of compelling and engaging app icons and screenshots.

4. Create an app description that is concise and to-the-point. Explain to consumers what problem your app solves and why it does the best job solving it. Make clear statements about your app's core features and how the app will benefit the consumer.

5. Another great tip is to try new names, categories, and keywords for your apps. This simple change can result in more downloads overnight.

6. Follow the Top Charts and track the trends on the App Store.

7. Read the reviews written for your app and make improvements that consumers want.

App Icon

The app icon is the most powerful tool in your marketing tool belt. A great app icon can be the deciding factor between a user downloading your app or looking for another. Download the app icons available at AppSchool.com/book. Then click the Choose File button.

Select the *iTunesArtwork.png* icon file. This icon is 1024x1024 px and will be used on the App Store.

Category

Selecting the correct App Store category is a very important piece of your app's marketing plan. Placing your app in the proper category will expose it to more users interested in your app.

Since this is a camera-based app, set the Primary Category to Photo & Video. Then review the options in the Secondary Category drop-down menu and select another category.

Rating

Rating information is used to guide parents and users toward content that is safe and encouraging. Apple asks for the level of different types of content. For example, Apple asks for the level of realistic violence inside your app. The Selfie app does not have any violence and should be set to None.

Click the Edit button next to Rating and evaluate the content qustions. Select None, Infrequent, or Frequent.

Trade Representative Contact Information

The App Store trade representative contact information is used in the Korean App Store. By Korean law, apps available for download must have a contact publicly associated with them. The following information is required and will be displayed only in Korea.

Enter the following representative information:

- First name
- Last name
- Email
- Address
- City

- State
- Postal code
- Country
- Phone number

Copyright

The copyright information is the year and person or entity that owns the rights to the app.

Enter your name followed by the year in the copyright input box.

App Review Information

The app review information is only sent to the App Review team (Figure 11-7). The App Review team may need to contact you about a particular feature or piece of your app. List your contact information inside the provided boxes.

Figure 11-7. App Review Information section

Enter the following information:

- First name
- Last name
- Phone number
- Email address

Demo account

In some cases, a demo account may be required for the app review. If there is any type of login or authentication inside your app, it is a good idea to provide a test account to the App Review team. This will ensure that they can see all of your app and will increase the chances of your app being approved.

Leave the demo account boxes empty for this app.

Notes

The notes section is used to tell the App Review team about certain things they might not notice or should know when using the app. This is a good place to provide additional details outside the description.

Leave the notes box empty for this app.

Version Release

The next section, titled Version Release, asks if the app version should be released to the App Store immediately after the app is approved. If not, the app can be manually released or scheduled for a specific day.

Mark "Automatically Release this Version" under the Version Release checkbox.

Languages

The App Store is available in 28 languages. The information provided should be adjusted to each language if possible. Otherwise, consumers will not see the app listing in their native language. Instead, they will see their app in English, a language they may or may not understand.

Scroll to the top and click English to see a drop-down menu of the other available languages.

Pricing

Scroll back to the top and open the Pricing tab. The next screen will ask for pricing and availability information (Figure 11-8):

Availability Date
> Set this to a date in the future if you would like your app to appear on the App Store on a specific day.

Price Tier
> Select the price for your app. Apple will take a 30% commission on all paid app sales.

Price Tier Effective Date
> Use the effective date to set a temporary price change.

Price Tier End Date
> End date for price change.

Discount for Education Institutions
> Offer education institution discounts with the Apple Volume Purchase Program.

Custom B2B App
> This is an option for Business to Business apps. The app will not be available publicly on the App Store if this option is enabled.

Territories
> Control which countries and territories will receive the app in their respective App Store.

iCloud Download Settings
> Control versions of the app that are available to download from iCloud.

Figure 11-8. Pricing

The availability date can be set to the future if you would like your app released on a particular date. For example, you may want to match your app's release with a marketing campaign beginning on a specific date.

Leave the availability date set to today, and the app will be released as soon as it is approved.

The Price Tier option manages the price charged to download your app. Price tiers are based on the US Dollar. Tier 1 is $0.99, Tier 2 is $1.99, and Tier 3 is $2.99. The equivalent amount will be charged in foreign countries.

Select Tier 0 and make this app free.

Discounts can be provided for education institutions since they typically buy in bulk. Check the box if you would like to enable discounts for education institutions. A Custom B2B App will be available only to Volume Purchase Program customers and not on the App Store.

Since this app is free, leave this box unselected.

Your app will be available in over 150 countries worldwide. If you would like to select which countries, click the Specific Territories link at the bottom of the page.

Leave the countries as they are and click Save then Cancel.

Uploading Your Binary

Once your app listing has been completed, click Save. Next, you upload your binary, also known as your *app*, to iTunes Connect.

Open your Xcode project file. In the toolbar at the top, click the device simulator drop-down menu and select iOS Device. This will ensure that the application is built for an actual device and not for the simulator. Next, from the top menu bar, click Product→Archive. The application will be built using the certificates and provisioning profiles specified. Once the application is done building, the Organizer will appear. The Organizer is available by clicking Window→Organizer from the top menu bar. With the Archives tab selected, a list of app archives will be shown.

Click the archived app and then click the Submit button at the top of the window. You may be prompted to provide your Apple ID and password. Select the app name and the App Store provisioning profile. Then click Submit. The application will then be analyzed and uploaded to iTunes Connect (Figure 11-9).

Figure 11-9. Uploading

The Build Section

The Build section is where you match applications you have uploaded to your app listing.

Open up the app listing inside iTunes Connect. Then scroll down to the Build section. Click the plus sign, then select the uploaded binary (Figure 11-10). If you don't see a plus sign and a message that reads "Click + to add a build before you submit your app," wait three to five minutes and refresh your listing. The Build section can be slow to update. Click Done, then scroll to the top and click Save.

Figure 11-10. Build

Ready for Submit

Your app listing is now complete. Scroll to the top and click Save then Submit for Review.

A set of questions will be displayed (Figure 11-11). Answer each question according to your app. The Selfie app is not designed to use cryptography or incorporate cryptography. The Selfie app does not contain third-party content. Finally, the Selfie app does not use the Advertising Identifier. Answer each question and click Save.

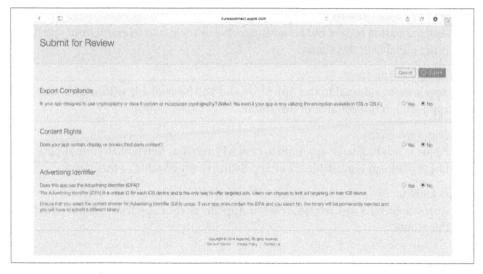

Figure 11-11. Submit

Statuses

Once the app listing has been submitted, your app's status will change to "Waiting for Review." Here is a list of all the possible app statuses. It is not necessary for your app to go through all these statuses. In most cases, an app will go from "Prepare for Submission" to "Waiting for Review" to "In Review" to "Processing for App Store" or "Rejected." You can view the entire status history for your application on the Status History page located at the bottom of the app listing page:

Prepare for Submission
App created in iTunes Connect, but not yet ready to be submitted for app review. Your app listing is still editable in this status.

Waiting for Review
App is waiting for review from the App Review team. There is no guaranteed time-frame for this status. Your app listing is still editable in this status.

In Review
App is currently being reviewed. There is no guaranteed timeframe for this status. Your app listing is not editable in this status.

Pending Contract
App has passed review, but contracts are not yet completed. Your app listing is not editable in this status.

Pending Developer Release

App has passed review, but is waiting on the developer to release it. Your app listing is not editable in this status.

Processing for App Store

App is being released to the App Store and will be available within 24 hours. Your app listing is not editable in this status.

Pending Apple Release

Apple is holding your app until a new iOS version. Verify that your application's target platform is available. Your app listing is not editable in this status.

Ready for Sale

App is approved and available on the App Store. Your app listing is not editable in this status.

Rejected

Apple has rejected the app; open the Resolution Center for more details. Your app listing is still editable in this status.

Metadata Rejected

The app listing items didn't pass the review. Correct your app listing info and re-submit. Your app listing is still editable in this status.

Removed from Sale

The app has been removed from sale by Apple. Apple will first contact you before removing your app from sale. Your app listing is not editable in this status.

Developer Rejected

You, the developer, have rejected the app. Your app listing is still editable in this status.

Developer Removed from Sale

You, the developer, have removed the app from the store. Your app listing is not editable in this status.

Invalid Binary

App provided didn't meet the upload requirements. Your app listing is still editable in this status.

App Review

Once your app has changed to In Review, your app will be reviewed by an Apple app reviewer. The review process can take anywhere from a few hours to a few days. The app reviewer will look to make sure your app is free of crashing and bugs. The app reviewer will also make sure the app matches the features listed in the app description. Finally, the app reviewer will make sure the app follows the Human Interface Guidelines (*http://bit.ly/1DT67XS*) and App Store Guidelines (*https://developer.apple.com/app-store/review/*).

App Rejection

Having an app rejected is part of learning to develop apps for the App Store. Do not think of rejection as a bad thing, but more as a learning opportunity. You can speak directly with the app reviewer inside the Resolution Center. Inside the Resolution Center, the app reviewer will explain which rule was broken. You can ask questions and get more specifics on how to fix the issues. Unfortunately, your app will go to the back of the line after a rejection, and you will have to wait again for your app to be reviewed.

App Approval

You will receive an email when your app changes to In Review. While most reviews are done the same day they start, this is not always the case. Most developers estimate around one week from the time they submit their app until app review is complete. If approved, your app will change to Processing for App Store. It can take up to 24 hours for your app to appear on the store. You will receive an email from iTunes Connect when your app is Ready for Sale.

CHAPTER 12

Managing and Marketing Your App

In this chapter, you will learn how to track downloads, review sales figures, update your app, and improve your marketing strategy. These techniques will take your app to the next level.

Tracking Sales and Downloads

Your work isn't over just because your app is on the App Store. Once an app is on the store, it should be managed and marketed appropriately. Monitoring downloads and sales is one of the most important metrics for your app. To monitor downloads and sales, you can use the Sales and Trends section inside iTunes Connect (*https://itunes connect.apple.com*).

The Sales and Trends section is updated everyday around 8 A.M. PST with the prior day's data. When you open the Sales and Trends section, a large graph will appear mapping the total number of units (downloads) for the specified time period. To view sales and revenue, click the Proceeds tab, and the graphs will update accordingly. You can also view your most popular territories and countries. This information can be especially helpful for translating and updating your app. The platform section of Sales and Trends will show you the device types used to download your app. You can export the data to CSV or XLS format using the small down arrow button in the upper-right corner. You can view daily, weekly, monthly, annual, and even lifetime reports containing your app statistics by clicking the drop-down menu in the upper-left corner and selecting Reports.

Payments and Financial Reports

iTunes Connect will also provide monthly reports containing total earnings and payments. These reports are more accurate than Sales and Trends, but are only calculated every month. You can view up to two years of payment history. Apple also provides detailed earnings reports; these can be helpful during end-of-the-year tax calculations.

To view the earnings and payment reports, click the "Payments and Financial Reports" section from the iTunes Connect home screen.

The Summary tab will show a breakdown of reported earnings for the previous month. The breakdown will include the total app sales for each country. Also, the "Payments and Amounts Owed" section will display the last payment made and the calculated amount for the upcoming payment. You can use the Trends graph at the bottom of the screen to map and track your payments month by month.

The Earnings tab will provide a breakdown of each country's revenue and downloads for each month. The country's revenue will be listed in the country's native currency. Click the Download button to download a financial report. The Owed tab will show the total revenue earned for each country and convert it into your local currency, i.e., US Dollars. The total amount owed for your next payment will be listed in the upper-right corner of the screen. This number is not final and will likely change before the payment date. Any products returned to Apple will be deducted from future payment. The payment amount shown already takes into consideration Apple's 30% commission on all sales.

The Payments tab shows detailed revenue, tax, and exchange rates. Payments take place 30 days after the month has ended. For example, January's earnings will be paid in the first week of March, February's earnings in the first week of April, etc.

Crashes

Your application may have bugs or not behave as expected in some cases. iTunes Connect provides customers' crash reports to the developer. These crash reports can be used to help locate and identify bugs inside your app. To view the crash report for a particular app, open the My Apps section of iTunes Connect. Next, click the desired app and then scroll to the bottom of the app listing. Under Additional Information, you will find Crash Reports. Click Download Report, and a *.crash* file will be provided. Double-click the *.crash* file to analyze the crash in Xcode.

Reviews

Nothing is more important than listening to your customers' feedback. The App Store reviews are a place where users can provide one to five stars and a brief description of your app. To view the reviews for your app, open the My Apps section in iTunes Connect. Select the desired app and then click Reviews at the top of the listing. The reviews will be displayed for the current version and separated by country. Change the country by using the drop-down menu in the upper-right corner. Read each customer's review and take into consideration what consumers like or dislike as a whole. Don't let one positive or negative review dictate your app. However, customer reviews should be the primary factor in determining what updates should be made to the app.

Updating Your App

While your app is on the store, you will learn more about your app. Your app will need to evolve to keep users happy. Updating your app is free for anyone who downloaded or purchased a previous version. There are many reasons to update your apps. For example, you might have new features, bug fixes, interface updates, etc. Adding a new version to your app is very similar to submitting your app to the App Store. App updates still follow the same review process as the first version.

App Updates and MetaData Changes

To add a new version, open the My Apps section of iTunes Connect and click the desired app. Click the New Version button in the upper-right corner of the screen. The new version detail page will be displayed. Fill out the new version number, i.e., 1.1, 1.2, and click Create. Then fill out the app listing information as you normally would. Be sure to fill out the "What's New in This Version" section. This message will be displayed in the Updates tab inside the App Store app.

Most app listing information can only be changed when an updated version is provided. Use this time to fix any errors in your app listing and make changes to your app's keywords and title if necessary. Once you are done, click Save and then "Submit for Review." Answer the legal and encryption questions, and you are ready to upload your updated version.

Promo Codes

Just because your app is listed on the App Store doesn't mean people will organically find it. To help potential costumers find your app, Apple provides promo codes. Promo codes are used to provide free access to a paid application. This can be extremely helpful when asking a blogger to review your app. You can request up to 100 promo codes for each version of your app. To request promo codes, open the My Apps section inside iTunes Connect. Click the desired app and then scroll to the bottom and click Promo Codes. The promo code page will appear. Enter the total number of promo codes you would like to generate and click Continue. Review the agreement and check if you agree; then click Continue. Click the blue Download button and a *.txt* file with the promo codes will be provided.

Analytics

The "Sales and Trends" section of iTunes Connect only provides download and revenue information. It would be helpful to understand how consumers are actually using your application. *What buttons are they pressing? How long is the app being used? Do the users come back after they use the app the first time?* All of these questions have valuable answers that will help you understand how your app is performing. Additional analytics packages are available from a variety of third-party sites. These services will provide a small snippet of code to go in your app. Once the snippet is added to your app, the analytics company will start collecting information about how your users behave. None of the information collected by the analytics provider will identify the user. The data collected is more detailed than the statistics provided by Apple in Sales and Trends.

Check out these free analytics providers:

- *http://www.flurry.com*
- *http://www.google.com/analytics/mobile/*
- *http://www.mixpanel.com*

Vanity URLs

You can create a link to your app in the App Store using Vanity URLs. Vanity URLs are used to create a memorable link to your app. They are extremely helpful in print advertising and for audio advertisements. To create a Vanity URL, take the company name or app name and append it to AppStore.com. For example, *http://www.appstore.com/ instagram* will link directly to Instagram on the App Store. Be sure to remove all spaces from the name and replace ampersands with *and*.

One More Thing

Congratulations, you made it! I hope you had fun on this journey from idea to App Store. But the journey is not over, this is just the beginning. Keep pushing the limits of your knowledge; the best way to learn something is to study something you want to learn. For example, want to learn more about Core Bluetooth? Check the documentation and try some Sample Code.

Remember, there will be tough times and fun times, but it is all worth it in the end. You will get stuck on a bug or issue, and it might feel like it is impossible to fix. These days are numbered, so just keep pushing and trying new things. Never give up. Before you know it, you will be laughing about the whole thing. You won't ever forget the solution to that issue again either.

Stay Hungry, Stay Foolish

Objective-C

 The material in this appendix is not required learning. However, since Swift is a new language, you are likely to see Objective-C code when building iOS Apps. This chapter provides some guidance on how to interact with Objective-C code.

In this appendix, you will learn about Objective-C. You will learn why should you know Objective-C and how to read Objective-C. These skills will prepare you for working with older code and guides.

Why Objective-C Still Matters

This book has taught you how to successfully go from idea to App Store, using Apple's newest programming language, Swift. Before Swift, Apple only had one official programming language, Objective-C. The Objective-C language was created by a team of software engineers at NEXT, a software and hardware company created by Steve Jobs after he was excused from Apple in the 1980s. Fortunately, in the 1990s Apple acquired NEXT along with Objective-C. The Objective-C language has served as the primary programming language for over 20 years. This language has been used for iOS programming since the first iOS SDK was released in 2008.

The iOS Stack

When an application is developed, it does not send messages directly to the hardware. Instead, Apple provides a series of layers that work together to translate the message to the hardware (Figure A-1).

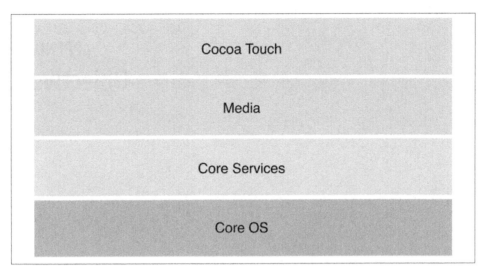

Figure A-1. Layers

The closest layer to the application is called *Cocoa Touch*. This means the application language, Swift, sends messages to the Cocoa Touch layer. The Cocoa Touch layer contains a series of frameworks and classes designed for development. The higher-level frameworks are simpler versions of the lower-level layers. The lower the layer, the more complex the source code. Remember, Swift talks directly to the Cocoa Touch layer. The Cocoa Touch layer provides the same classes and frameworks available in Objective-C.

How to Read Objective-C

It's important to understand how to read Objective-C, because most iOS classes, frameworks, and documentation are still written in Objective-C. Initializing an object in Objective-C looks like this:

```
UIViewController *myViewController = [[UIViewController alloc] init];
```

Initializing an object in Swift looks like this:

```
var myViewController = UIViewController()
```

The Objective-C language is accomplishing the same task, but with more code. The Objective-C version uses brackets. These brackets act like parentheses in a math equation. The innermost set of brackets executes first and then the result is used as part of the next statement. In Objective-C, variables are created with a specific type. For example:

```
UIViewController *myViewController
```

This line creates a variable using a pointer, but the variable name is the same.

In Objective-C, brackets are used to send a message; a message tells a particular class or object to do something. Message syntax looks like this:

```
[subject verb]
```

The brackets are used at the beginning and end of the message. The first item in the message is the subject. The subject is the object or class that will receive the message. The subject is followed by a space and then a verb. This verb is usually a method or function. The method can also take parameters like this:

```
[subject verb:parameter]
```

A colon is used to delineate between the method and parameter. Review the following line of Objective-C:

```
UIViewController *myViewController = [[UIViewController alloc] init];
```

From left to right, a `UIViewController` variable is created named `myViewController`. The variable is then set to the output from the right side of the statement. The right side of the statement starts with [`UIViewController alloc`]. This `alloc` method is used to allocate memory for the newly formed object. Next, the newly formed memory is passed to `init`. The `init` method initializes the memory and creates a new `UIView Controller` object. Finally, the `myViewController` variable is set to the newly created `UIViewController` object.

This syntax may not feel natural at first, but you don't have to master it. The semicolon at the end of each line works like a period at the end of a sentence and declares the end of the statement.

Properties in Objective-C work in a very similar manner as Swift. Instead of using a message, you can get and set a property using a dot, just like in Swift:

Objective-C
```
myLabel.text = @"Steve"
```

Swift
```
myLabel.text = "Steve"
```

Both languages follow the same pattern, subject dot property and then equals sign. The only difference in this example is the @ sign used before a string in Objective-C. Otherwise, the two languages are very similar.

You may have noticed another difference when working with Objective-C files. Objective-C classes are made up of two separate files. The two files work together as a pair: *.h* and *.m*. The *.h* file is known as the *header*. The header file lists all the public methods and properties for the class. The *.m* file contains the code that executes the methods and properties displayed in the header. Think of the *.h* like the menu at a restaurant and the *.m* like the kitchen. You can see what is available in the *.h* file, and you don't have to go back to the kitchen to see how it's made.

Aside from a few syntax differences, Swift and Objective-C are very similar. They both talk to Cocoa and Cocoa Touch, so their underlying interfaces are the same. With a little practice, you can learn to read and write Objective-C from your Swift experience. Stick with Swift and learn Objective-C if you have a legitimate reason. Keep practicing and pushing your limits each and every day.

List of Synonyms

- Instance and object
- Data and information
- Parameter and input
- Return value and output
- Attribute, property, characteristic, and trait
- Behavior, method, and function

Index

We'd like to hear your suggestions for improving our indexes. Send email to index@oreilly.com.

requesting, 215–217

About the Author

Steve Derico is the founder and lead iOS Developer at Bixby Apps. Bixby Apps is a mobile app development agency located in San Francisco. Bixby Apps builds top-rated apps used worldwide by millions and works with Fortune 500 clients like BMW, Lenovo, and MGM Resorts. You can find their work at *http://www.bixbyapps.com*.

Steve is also the founder and iOS Professor at App School. App School is an online app development school for absolute beginners. No programming experience is required. App School has taught hundreds of nonprogrammers how to make apps. You can learn how to make apps at *http://www.appschool.com*.

Steve enjoys wine, baseball, and running in his free time. He also loves to hear from readers and answer their questions. You can reach him at *steve@appschool.com*, *http://www.twitter.com/stevederico*, or (415) 779-2771.

Colophon

The animal on the cover of *Introducing iOS 8* is Goeldi's marmoset (*Callimico goeldii*), a small South American monkey (about the size of a squirrel) that lives in the upper Amazon Basin region of Bolivia, Brazil, Colombia, Ecuador, and Peru. The species takes its name from its discoverer, the Swiss naturalist Emil August Goeldi.

Goeldi's marmosets are blackish or blackish-brown and the hair on their head and tail sometimes has red, white, or silvery brown highlights. Their bodies are about 8–9 inches long, and their tails are about 10–12 inches long. They live in small social groups (approximately six individuals) that stay within a few feet of one another most of the time, staying in contact via high-pitched calls.

Goeldi's marmosets prefer to forage in dense scrubby undergrowth; perhaps because of this, they are fairly rare. In the wet season, their diet includes fruit, insects, spiders, lizards, frogs, and snakes. In the dry season, they feed on fungi—they are the only tropical primates known to depend on this source of food.

Many of the animals on O'Reilly covers are endangered; all of them are important to the world. To learn more about how you can help, go to *animals.oreilly.com*.

The cover image is from Lydekker's *Royal Natural History*. The cover fonts are URW Typewriter and Guardian Sans. The text font is Adobe Minion Pro; the heading font is Adobe Myriad Condensed; and the code font is Dalton Maag's Ubuntu Mono.

Have it your way.

Get even more for your money.

Join the O'Reilly Community, and register the O'Reilly books you own. It's free, and you'll get:

- $4.99 ebook upgrade offer
- 40% upgrade offer on O'Reilly print books
- Membership discounts on books and events
- Free lifetime updates to ebooks and videos
- Multiple ebook formats, DRM FREE
- Participation in the O'Reilly community
- Newsletters
- Account management
- 100% Satisfaction Guarantee

Signing up is easy:

1. Go to: oreilly.com/go/register
2. Create an O'Reilly login.
3. Provide your address.
4. Register your books.

Note: English-language books only

To order books online:
oreilly.com/store

For questions about products or an order:
orders@oreilly.com

To sign up to get topic-specific email announcements and/or news about upcoming books, conferences, special offers, and new technologies:
elists@oreilly.com

For technical questions about book content:
booktech@oreilly.com

To submit new book proposals to our editors:
proposals@oreilly.com

O'Reilly books are available in multiple DRM-free ebook formats. For more information:
oreilly.com/ebooks

O'REILLY®

CPSIA information can be obtained at www.ICGtesting.com
Printed in the USA
BVOW09s2250250115

384877BV00011B/44/P